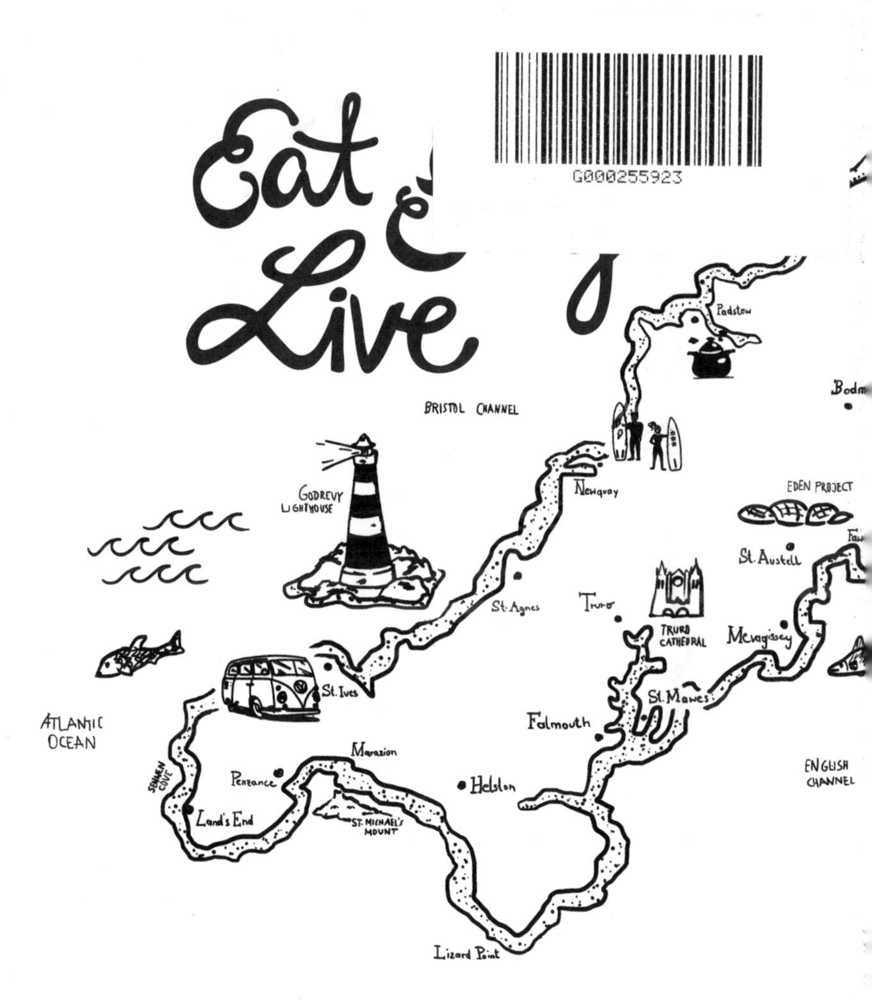

THE CORNWALL TRAVEL BOOK

VERA BACHERNEGG
KATHARINA MARIA ZIMMERMANN

EAT SURF LIVE

This edition published in 2018 by Summersdale Publishers Ltd.

First published by Eat Write Live in 2016

Map © Georg Liebergesell
Design by Verena Jauk, Verena Michelitsch, Christina Michelitsch
Illustrations by Georg Liebergesell, Verena Jauk, Katharina Maria Zimmermann
Photographs by Katharina Maria Zimmermann, Vera Bachernegg (pp.35, 270, 271), Harris Rothschild (p.185), Matt Smith (p.221), Marion Luttenberger (pp.274, 276), Melanie Kraxner (p.275)

An Hachette UK Company
www.hachette.co.uk

Summersdale Publishers Ltd
Part of Octopus Publishing Group Limited
Carmelite House
50 Victoria Embankment
LONDON
EC4Y 0DZ
UK

www.summersdale.com

Printed and bound in China

ISBN: 978-1-78685-262-5

INTRODUCTION

Until 2009 we had no plans to visit Cornwall in the southwest of England. That quickly changed when we entered the county for the first time. We did not know what to expect, but we were blown away (quite literally!) and could hardly believe our eyes: there, across the English Channel, was a place full of young people, sexy surfers, marvellous shops and restaurants whose offerings made our tastebuds and stomachs explode with joy. Somewhere around this time *Eat Surf Live* was born; we had to share this place with the world!

We knew from the start that we wanted to distance ourselves from classical guidebooks. We are more about looking behind the scenes and showing what is really going on in Cornwall. Through interviews and stories, we found out what makes the Cornish tick. How do they think? What do they eat, drink or snack on? What is there to do and experience? And above all: what do the locals recommend to first-time visitors? We take a close look at the vibrant lifestyle lurking in every corner and also get to know some old and delicious recipes. We are fascinated by this region and don't want you to miss any of it!

Eat Surf Live: the Cornwall Travel Book is about making the most of Cornwall: traditional recipes as well as idiosyncratic and new English cuisine. It's about sport: riding waves, hiking on the South West Coast Path, coasteering, climbing and more. Above all it is about the people.

So have fun on your journey of discovery in this exceptional corner of the world with

Eat Surf Live!

Best wishes,
Vera Bachernegg &
Katharina Maria Zimmermann

CONTENTS

CHAPTER 1 – FROM RAME TO THE EDEN PROJECT

CHAPTER 2 – TRURO, FALMOUTH, ROSELAND & THE LIZARD

CHAPTER 3 – THE PENWITH PENINSULA

CHAPTER 4 – ST IVES

CHAPTER 5 – THE NORTH

GENERAL

A MINI

ABC of Cornwall

FOR BEGINNERS & EXPERTS

IF YOU HAVEN'T YET TRAVELLED TO THE SOUTH OF ENGLAND, HERE IS A QUICK AND EASY OVERVIEW. LEARN SOME VOCABULARY AND GUESS THE MEANING. YOU WILL ALSO FIND OUT WHAT MAKES THE BRITS IN THE WILD SOUTHWEST TICK.

A for Arthur, King Arthur.

Many myths and legends surround King Arthur and his Knights of the Round Table. His birthplace still remains a mystery to this day. However, one legend does mention that he was born in Tintagel Castle in Cornwall. Today you can not only visit the castle ruins, but also the nearby supposed cave of Merlin the Wizard.

B for Breakfast.

If you don't care for 'full English breakfasts', then let us assure you that there are alternatives in several places, such as homemade jams, mueslis, wholegrain toast and fruit.

Anyway, if the locals are to be believed, you cannot leave Cornwall without trying smoked haddock or kippers for breakfast.

C for Cider.

Going to Cornwall without drinking cider is like a trip to Bordeaux without wine, that is to say, practically impossible. There are already many local producers who place a particular emphasis on organically grown apples. Try it!

D for Dainty.

Cornwall is not urban. The largest city is St Austell with approximately 20,000 inhabitants. But this is exactly what makes Cornwall so charming: narrow streets which stop any speed freaks and a small, but fine, variety of exceptional shops which means a day-long shopping spree is not on the cards. The idea is to be outside (maybe even in the rain once or twice), and to experience the country as well as the people.

E for Easy to Get to.

A nice and relaxed way of travelling to Cornwall is by railway. Trains run regularly from London Paddington, as well as Gatwick Airport, to the south of England. Altogether there are 36 train stations in Cornwall that can be accessed. The advantage: not having to drive on the left if you are not used to it.

F for Fistral Beach.

This beach and its waves are famous to surfers both abroad and at home. Fittingly, surfing contests are held here. This means the beach is slightly overcrowded and only recommendable to those who like a bustling atmosphere in the water. Cornwall has many other more peaceful spots to offer: Kennack Sands for example.

G for Grog and Pirates.

The latter in particular were common in Cornwall for a long time. The village

of Polperro served as a stronghold for smugglers. The Jamaica Inn became known as the premier spot for smugglers to meet near Bodmin Moor. Today the only pirates left may be the local rugby team, the Cornish Pirates.

H for Holy Cow, That's Cold!

The water in Cornwall is not exactly known for its excessively high temperatures, which you may notice when swimming or surfing. If this doesn't scare you off, you might even become a fan of the so-called 'Christmas Day Swim'.

I for Isles of Scilly.

Those who want to let the wonderful landscape and beaches work their magic calmly are in the right place 45 kilometres southwest of Land's End, in the Scilly Isles. The near-subtropical climate, palms and sunshine are mouth-watering. There are a few flight and transport connections available to reach this family of islands from the mainland.

J for Junior.

No – we're not talking junior suite but rather youth hostel. Along with the usual camping, hostels are another cheap alternative to hotels in the area. The Boscastle Youth Hostel comes to mind particularly for Coast Path hikers, as well as the Youth Hostel Coverack with its great view of the sea; or the Perranporth Youth Hostel, which is ideal for surfing enthusiasts.

K for Kernowek.

The Celtic language of Cornish (Kernowek) was nearly extinct but is now experiencing its renaissance. If you are confused by the place names, the Celts are to blame!

L for Lost Gardens of Heligan.

In Cornwall it is hard to resist visiting one of the old country estates with their well-maintained gardens. One option would be the Lost Gardens of Heligan, another the well-known Trebah Garden. These spots are as representative of the county as Fistral Beach or the South West Coast Path. Plain

and simply, this is why Cornwall is called 'the Garden Capital of the World'.

M for Meur ras (Say: murrAS).

Means 'Thank you' in Cornish. You can certainly score points with the locals by using this.

N for Newquay.

Known across England as a Mecca for surfers. No doubt due to its youthful allure, it is also a popular venue for stag dos and hen nights. From spring to summer, there is one raucous party after the next – everyone living life to the full! If you are looking to party, then this is your town. The Cornish who do not live in Newquay however, do not have the most positive opinion of this surf metropolis. We say: it's better you make up your own mind. Beaches such as Fistral Beach or Lusty Glaze Beach are great; in the Chy Bar it is easy to hang out with the locals and the surfing shops offer cool clothes.

O for Cornish Orchards.

Cornish Orchards have seen how powerful a change of label can be. They have always produced good apple juice and excellent cider near Looe, however this has only been noticed by visitors to most restaurants and cafés since the redesign. We suggest the Blush raspberry cider, which can be bought cheaply at the shops.

P for Porth-.

Porthminster, Porthmeor, Porthchapel, Porth Beach. 'Porth' is a regional Cornish word meaning small bay or cove. This list of names beginning with Porth and describing beautiful beaches could go on forever. What's important for visitors to Cornwall: if a beach begins with Porth, then it has something to offer.

Q for Quirky.

Odd, strange, peculiar, those are the Cornish. Do we think they're funny and charming? Yes! They believe in ghosts and elves, are basically married to their dogs and even go surfing in February. That shows character.

R for Riddles.

There are Treasure Trails all over Cornwall. These are mini maps, packed full of puzzles, just waiting to be picked up by holidaymakers and adventurers – leading to tiny villages and hidden corners that you definitely would never have discovered without Treasure Trails. These mini puzzles and riddles have been hidden for you to solve. Loads of fun!

S for Signs.

The signs the Cornish write their house names on are lovely. Sometimes ornate, sometimes quite modest, they name the dwellings and cottages. Their treachery is only discovered when you are getting around with satnav, as only then do you realise that very few houses in Cornwall are numbered. This tiny but tricky detail makes looking for accommodation, a good café or a terrific restaurant even more exciting.

T for Tre-.

'By Tre, Pol and Pen shall ye know all Cornishmen' said Richard Carew in 1602. It still rings true today. These prefixes can be seen in any kind of name. No wonder, as they stand for settlement (Tre), pond (Pol) or hill (Pen).

U for Undulating.

Waves are a common theme in this surfing-mad corner of the world, whether they are calmly undulating or crashing wildly.

V for Veryan.

Despite being inland and away from the sea (or perhaps because of it!), this village is mesmerizing. This gem lies at the heart of the Roseland Peninsula. Time seems to have come to a standstill here. A must-see for romantics.

W for Water.

The Cornish live on the water's edge. They can hardly help it. You don't need to drive far before you suddenly arrive at the next cliff-adorned coast. Detractors say: Cornwall is a frame without a picture. We say: there are beautiful sights inland as well, but it is surely the coasts that bewitch visitors.

X for XXX.

Cornwall is so beautiful and inspiring that you'll easily fall in love with the county and its people. The authors of this book even wrote a love-letter to St Ives, which they've ended with the three obligatory Xs.

Y for Cornish Yarg.

Yarg sounds like a pirate's cry: Yarrrgggggh! It is actually the name Gray (the inventor of Yarg), simply spelt backwards. Yarg is a white cheese packed in nettles, that generally tastes slightly of garlic. It is however thoroughly recommendable and available in any good deli.

Z for The End of the World (or the End of the ABC).

This is true for Cornwall: the westernmost as well as the southernmost points of Britain are found in Cornwall. At the same time, Land's End and Lizard Point are not that far away from each other. If you wish to visit one of these points, go to Lizard Point. It is somehow much more real and authentic than the artificial theme park that has been built around Land's End. The most sensible option at Land's End is definitely a walk or a small hike on the South West Coast Path that snakes along the coast of Cornwall.

FROM Rame TO THE Eden Project

Getting started! The untouched peninsula, the alluring Looe, the sailing-mad Fowey, the pirate and smugglers' nest Polperro and the widely known Eden Project – together with many others – are the stations of this chapter. A great place to start exploring Cornwall.

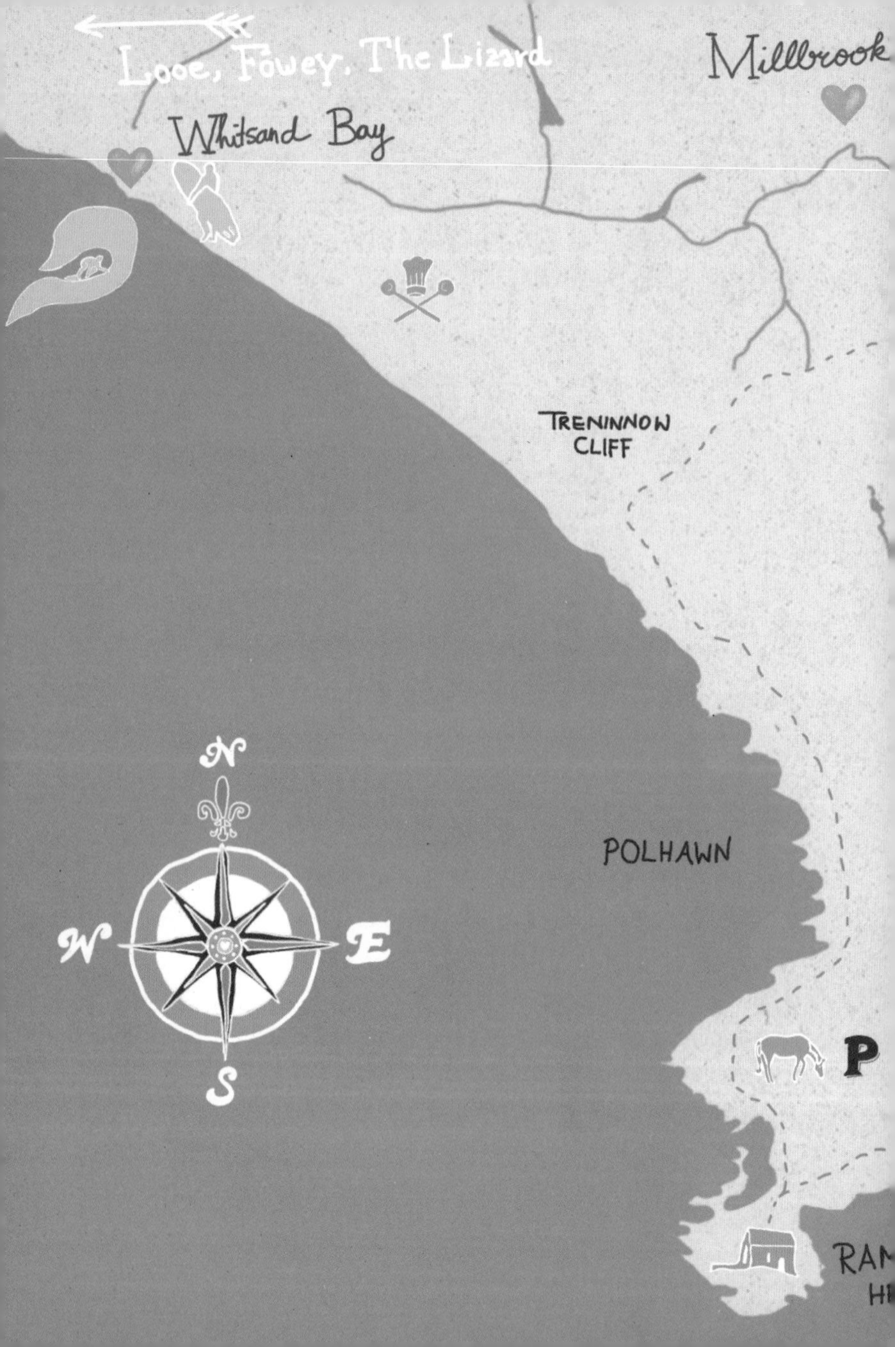
Looe, Fowey, The Lizard
Millbrook
Whitsand Bay
TRENINNOW
CLIFF
POLHAWN
N
W
E
S

PIGSHILL WOOD

Devon

CLARRICK WOODS

Maker

Kingsand

P

Cawsand

P

ENGLISH CHANNEL

Rame

PENLEE

P

RAME PENINSULA

AROUND RAME HEAD

IF YOU WANT A VIEW OF THE SOUTH WEST COAST PATH, OLD CHURCHES AND A CEMETERY BY THE SEA, THEN TAKE A WALK ALONG THE POINTY NOSE OF THE 'FORGOTTEN PENINSULA' RAME.

Why wouldn't you build a church in this delightful place? That was the first question we asked ourselves as Rame Head, the furthest point of the Rame Peninsula, emerged in front of us. When we arrived at the ancient St Michael's Chapel, out of breath, the question had changed: why on earth would you build a church HERE? Who, unless they have decided on a long walk, visits this place? As the path also leads to the slightly newer and nearer Rame Church, we knew that we were apparently not the only ones, and definitely not the first, to entertain these thoughts. Incidentally, there is a truly Cornish cemetery surrounding the church, with a view of the sea and anchors on the gravestones.

Rame Church is also a very popular place to get married, as it isn't connected to the electricity grid yet and therefore relies on candlelight, which is extremely romantic.

AS A STARTER

The path around Rame that leads you from Kingsand right back to Kingsand can be seen as a 'starter' in two ways. Not only is Rame a perfect place to start a holiday in Cornwall but this approx one and a half to three hour tour (depending on walking pace) is also an ideal introduction to the Cornish hiking paradise, with its nearly 1,000 kilometre long South West Coast Path and numerous hiking trails in-between.

This route covers everything a hiker in Cornwall could desire: a view of the sea, overgrown paths and wild horses. What's more, the panorama you can enjoy at Rame Head is simply incredible. You can see as far as the Lizard Peninsula to the West, and in the East, Plymouth glitters grandly in the distance.

PICTURE PERFECT

At the southernmost point of the Rame Peninsula you can, as stated in our hiking tour, go to Rame Head. On the way there, just after the car park (if you don't hike the whole way from Kingsand, you can park relatively close to Rame Head), you come to an area with wild, quintessentially Cornish ponies. In combination with the deep blue sea, these make excellent subjects for photographic experimentation. If you've brought a telephoto lens with you, you will be able to take absolutely fantastic photos of the Lizard Peninsula and the surrounding cliffs.

Bill Bryson

KINGSAND AND CAWSAND

THE TWIN TOWN

KINGSAND, CAWSAND, AREN'T THEY JUST THE SAME THING? ALTHOUGH WE ARE STILL NOT ENTIRELY SURE, WE CAN TELL YOU THAT THE RAME PENINSULA IS CERTAINLY NOT BORING! THAT WORD WOULD NOT DO JUSTICE TO THE TWIN PEARLS KINGSAND AND CAWSAND AND THE CALL OF A FORGOTTEN PENINSULA.

That Kingsand and Cawsand don't get the attention they deserve is perhaps due to the fact that most visitors are magnetically attracted to the 'big city' of Plymouth and thereby forget to notice just how lovely, simple and rustically maritime these two tiny towns are. These two places are practically one (the border is in a house!) but live in constant competition with one another. 'We have a nice story; Kingsand was home to the King's tax collectors, hence the name. The Cawsanders simply invented a story for the tourists about the origin of their town's name,' says Bruce who, unsurprisingly, was born in Kingsand. Most accommodation comes with a view of the sea, such as Westcroft Guesthouse, where you can even see the sea from the toilet (a loo with a

view!). It is also a pleasure to lie in bed and fall asleep to the lapping of the waves. Apart from that, Kingsand is a traditional town with the narrowest streets, a few pubs and restaurants, plus lots of fishermen and locals who know each other, as well as an annual Christmas Swim (Cawsand is too but the Kingsanders would never admit it to us!). If you want to visit the beach, then you can go directly to the one in Kingsand, the one in Cawsand (who'd have thought?) or drive a few minutes to Whitsand Bay. By the way, the reason as to why the two towns have such a split personality: until 1844 they were actually in two different counties. Cawsand was in Cornwall, Kingsand in Devon.

FOOD LOVER

TOO GOOD TO EVER FORGET

WE KNOW THE STORY OF THE FORGOTTEN PENINSULA RAME, AND WE HAVE TO SAY: IT'S YOUR OWN FAULT IF YOU MISS OUT ON IT! THIS IS A REALLY GOOD PLACE TO EAT. HERE'S THE TOP 4 AT A GLANCE:

THE OLD BOATSTORE CAFÉ

Where man and dog meet for coffee lies the Old Boatstore Café. Inside there is tea and coffee that can be taken outside to the benches at the water's edge. Here you can forge your plans for the day and praise the day's good weather (if it lives up to expectations that is), otherwise you can sit quietly or talk about the last nice day. Inside you can order a build-your-own breakfast per ingredient (such as baked beans or toast, for 50 pence). There are also American pancakes or a few lunch dishes available.

THE CLEAVE, KINGSAND, PL10 1NF
TEL. 01752 822036
WWW.THEOLDBOATSTORE.CO.UK

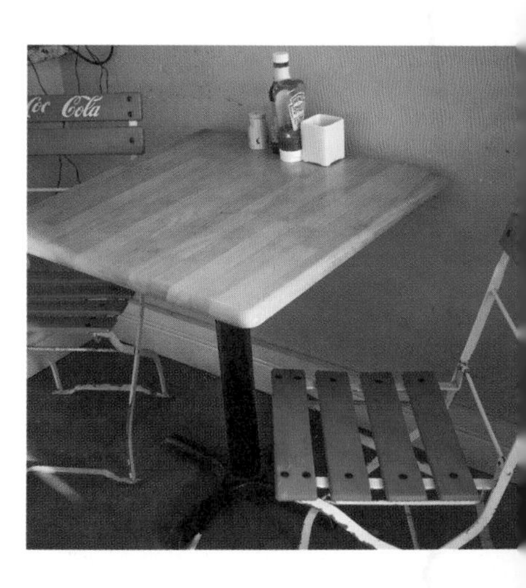

THE VIEW RESTAURANT

Beware: the owner Matt is a genuine surfer and when the surf looks good on Whitsand Bay, he sometimes closes his restaurant, packs his surfboard and says goodbye for a few hours. This reflects not only the surfing culture but also the entire atmosphere of Rame Peninsula. Other than that, when Matt is working, the view here is the name of the game. There is indeed a fantastic panorama of the bay and the endless ocean. This seems to make the seafood taste even better. Incidentally, this restaurant, with its huge windows, is as popular with the locals as the Devonport Inn. Although you do have to drive slightly further, and there is always the possibility that Matt has traded his chopping board for his surfboard.

TRENNINOW CLIFF ROAD
TORPOINT, PL10 1JY
TEL. 01752 822345
WWW.THEVIEW-RESTAURANT.CO.UK

THE DEVONPORT INN

Dawn & Jerome Leopold run everybody's favourite pub here in Kingsand. It's situated directly on the promenade, which is already sun-kissed when the head chef walks his dog early in the morning. Later, aromas of freshly baked bread, delicious seafood or French classics billow out of the kitchen. The first guests come at noon, when the large blackboard reveals what is on the menu for lunch (£6–10). The starters range from bombs (warm Camembert) to traditional dishes (chicken liver with bacon), to fresh sea goodies (smoked salmon). But it is the main course that crowns a visit to the Devonport Inn: steak, scallops or risotto with truffles for the veggies. For anyone wanting to lose themselves in the view of the ocean in the afternoon or evening, there is some bad news: the best tables can't be booked no matter how hard you try. You just need to be lucky. In the evening the shack is packed, but even when you can't get hold of a table, we recommend waiting at the counter and enjoying a Pimm's or swigging an ale. It's really worth it!

THE CLEAVE, KINGSAND, PL10 1NF
TEL. 01752 822869
WWW.DEVONPORTINN.COM

THE CANTEEN

The Maker Heights' hill alone would be worth the trip, as the view is beautiful and the fresh air does you good. And then there is the café-restaurant Canteen. It is nestled in a former Nissen hut (a corrugated iron hut with a semicircular roof) and offers space both inside and out to sit down and try the refreshing menu. Soups, curries, pulled pork burgers or crunchy salad dishes decorate the handwritten board, and delight locals as well as visitors to Cornwall. The motto is fittingly 'Do lovely things with beautiful local produce'.

MAKER HEIGHTS
MILLBROOK, PL10 1LA
TEL. 01752 659069
FACEBOOK.COM/MAKERCANTEEN

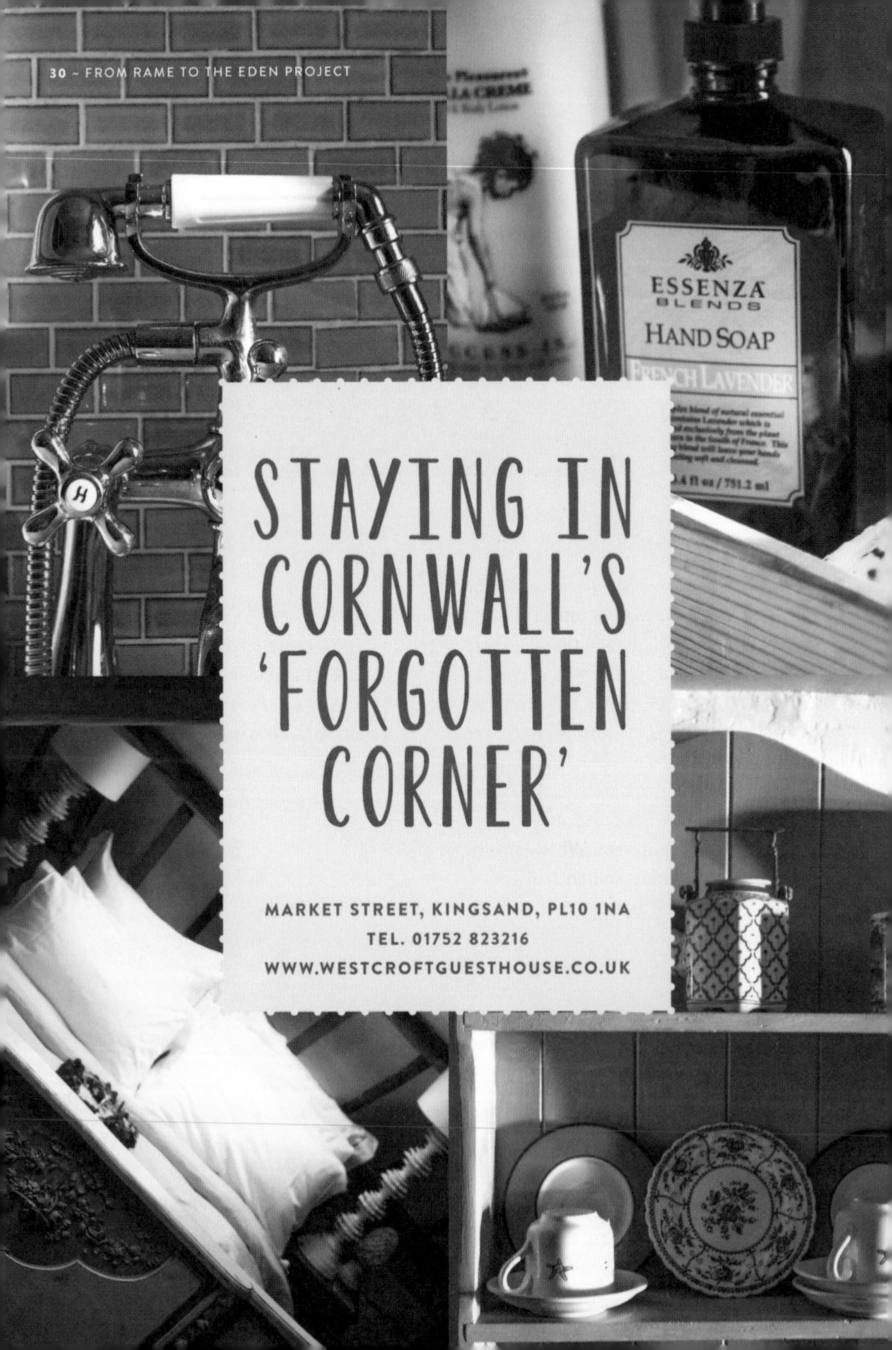
ESSENZA
BLENDS
HAND SOAP
FRENCH LAVENDER
STAYING IN
CORNWALL'S
'FORGOTTEN
CORNER'
MARKET STREET, KINGSAND, PL10 1NA
TEL. 01752 823216
WWW.WESTCROFTGUESTHOUSE.CO.UK

TUCKED AWAY IN A SMALL, BUZZING CORNISH VILLAGE: SARAH AND DYLAN'S WESTCROFT GUESTHOUSE

Dylan & Sarah

Westcroft is not just a guesthouse, it's also a gallery. This makes Westcroft a hub of action in Kingsand year in, year out. The small courtyard is always buzzing with activity: a curious visitor peeking at the gallery here or a friend dropping in to say hello there. Westcroft offers various types of accommodation: firstly, the well-designed rooms in the guesthouse and secondly, the rustic Shell Cottage – complete with an open fireplace. Thirdly, artists live in the flat above the gallery to become inspired by Kingsand and hold art courses. Every room in the guesthouse is different. What's unique is that Sarah and Dylan match the perfect room to the guest through a telephone conversation, or they offer the entire house for self-catering.

DON'T FORGET TO TAKE A BREAK(FAST)

If you are not self-catering and have booked the B&B, you will start the day with yoghurt and strawberries. Afterwards, fresh fruit, breads and jams are at the ready. The next course: eggs, bacon, mushrooms and grilled cherry tomatoes on the vine, 'a beautiful way to make an English breakfast'. Particularly charming: the square in front of the Westcroft is more or less the centre of the tiny village of Kingsand. If you partake of a cup of tea or a glass of Pimm's, you'll hear Sarah exclaim delightedly, 'Just like the locals!'

SPECIAL TIPS FROM SARAH & DYLAN

THE CAREW ARMS
(NEAR TORPOINT)

~

THE FREATHY FARMHOUSE
(NEAR MILLBROOK)

~

'You need fresh eyes to see the obvious.'

SARAH

ACTION HERO

IN YOGA LIES THE POWER

Emma Mansfield

She was a book-writing fact-lover. A yoga-teaching Cornwall fangirl. When Emma's stressful times in TV production, at the BBC and as a creative producer at the Eden Project were finished, her love for Cornwall could take over. As a result, she has made many declarations of love for the place in book form, as well as in her yoga courses and music.

Inhale, exhale. Repeat. I have never paid so much attention to breathing. What? It's good for you. Now it's time to stick your behind in the air, get on your knees and then do the same thing all over again. This is my yoga premiere in the middle of the Bodmin Dragon Leisure Centre. I'm not doing too badly. At least I don't think so. I only begin to feel its effects a day later, as nothing can get to me, not even narrow roads or stressful situations. Emma Mansfield's yoga shield has surrounded me. I have never been so peaceful. But somehow something stirs in me: I want more!

This is probably what Emma thought when she was caught by the yoga bug in Cornwall and could not rest until she had completed the training qualification. Now she gives various classes (even on the beach!). What's more, this superwoman has plenty under her belt. Plus a sheer, inexhaustible energy that she puts into writing trivia books such as *The Little Book of Cornwall* or *The Little Book of Clay Country*, as well as running various choirs in Lostwithiel.

WWW.LOVELYYOGACORNWALL.COM

PAUL THE POTTER

A FEW YEARS AGO PAUL AND HIS WIFE KAREN MOVED INTO AN EIGTHTEENTH-CENTURY FARMHOUSE, THEN GAVE IT A NEW SPARKLE AND A NEW FUNCTION: HOSTING HOLIDAYMAKERS AND OFFERING POTTERY WORKSHOPS.

Paul & Karen

At Rame Barton, Karen is responsible for the B&B and the self-catering flats. Meanwhile Paul runs his 'monster' in the studio, next to the old farmhouse. During Paul's professional artistic career he created many designs – in particular teapots for Disney and the famous piggy banks for NatWest Bank. Nowadays the famous potter is more relaxed.

The great thing is you can get creative yourself and put your hands to the potter's wheel. So have fun potting with Mr Cardew (you can register any time!).

Paul used to be a surfer, and remarks jokingly that he stopped the moment he realised he would never surf like his nephew Tom Lowe, professional big wave surfer and World Surf League competition finalist. As he could never really tear himself away from the water, he introduced the Christmas Day Swims to Kingsand, an event where the Cornish plunge into the wintry cold seas.

Paul is also a jack of all trades: he gladly prepares the guests' accommodation if Karen is busy or elsewhere. And there is no issue with spur-of-the-moment pottery making!

PAUL'S TIPS :

THE DEVONPORT INN

—

LUNCH AT THE VIEW

—

SURFING AND EVERYTHING ELSE ON WHITSAND BAY

TORPOINT, PL10 1LG
TEL. 01752 822789
WWW.RAMEBARTON.CO.UK

THINK TWICE

BOTELET FARM

NEAR LISKEARD YOU CAN EXPERIENCE HOW NATURAL AND INSPIRING LIFE IN HARMONY WITH THE ELEMENTS CAN BE, ON A LARGE PIECE OF LAND THE TAMBLYN FAMILY HAS OWNED FOR GENERATIONS.

AT BOTELET, PART OF THE FAMILY'S OLD FARMHOUSE WAS REMODELLED INTO A B&B IN THE 1930S. TWO COTTAGES ARE AVAILABLE IF YOU WANT TO GO SELF-CATERING. THERE ARE ALSO YURTS WHERE YOU CAN UNPACK YOUR CAMPING EQUIPMENT IN A FLOWERY MEADOW.

On the farm there is a deep understanding of man and nature – and it's always been this way – not simply since it has been 'in' to exhibit a green conscience and to be careful to eat healthy foods. Today that means:

seasonal, regional products for breakfast: yoghurt, homemade muesli, homemade bread, nuts, dried fruit and much more.

Eighty per cent of the electricity is produced by the two newly built wind turbines and solar panels.

No mass production, no insecticides.

For generations it has been natural to live economically and using as few resources as possible.

The tiered pricing was created as an incentive to stay longer than one night, in order to save energy on daily changes in bed linen and laundry, etc.

So everything is like an organic farm. However Botelet doesn't hang up an organic sign, as the farm would rather remain unregistered (and also make its grassland available to non-organic farmers from the area). For this reason they are listed in the Countryside Stewardship Scheme, which is dedicated to preserving English farmland and the species that live there.

JULIE'S TIPS:

Once a year watch the Polo on the Beach at Watergate Bay.

SURFING ON POLZEATH BEACH.

Reserve a table at The Plough near Duloe and experience a culinary highlight.

Julie

Visit St Tudy Inn in the North of Cornwall.

OUR TIPS:

Reserve yurts and sleep as if you were in Mongolia.

Polmartin Farm for riding enthusiasts.

NEED A MASSAGE? Tia Tamblyn (Julie's sister-in-law) is a master of massage.

BOTELET, PL14 4RD

TEL. 01503 220225, STAY@BOTELET.COM, WWW.BOTELET.COM

V R
POST OFFICE
Collections

CREAM TEA AT HOME

Scones & Clotted Cream

Scones and clotted cream are a part of Cornwall as much as the wind and the sea. Here is Julie Tambyln's recipe so you can celebrate teatime from the comfort of your own home.

CORNISH SPLITS

*

450 G WHITE FLOUR
60 G BUTTER
1 TEASPOON SALT
1 TEASPOON WHITE SUGAR
7 G DRIED YEAST
280 ML WARM MILK (45°C)

*

Tip: You can also use golden syrup instead of jam. These two together are called 'thunder and lightning'.

Put the flour, salt and sugar in a large bowl. Then stir in the yeast. Rub the butter into the mix until it resembles small breadcrumbs. Make a small well and add the milk, mix, then knead for 5–10 minutes. Cover and leave in a warm place to rise. It should rise to twice its size.

Knead again and form a dozen balls. Put on a baking tray and leave to rise again. Pre-heat the oven to 200°C (slightly lower for a fan-oven), leave the splits to bake for 15–20 minutes. Leave on a cooling rack. Cut or tear through the middle and serve with jam and clotted cream.

SCALD (CLOTTED) CREAM

*

2 LITRES OF MILK
(WITH THE HIGHEST FAT PERCENTAGE YOU CAN FIND, IDEALLY NON-HOMOGENISED)

*

In order to make the famous Cornish clotted cream, you need a milk centrifuge. Since very few people actually have one, Julie tells us how to make scald cream from 'normal' milk.

To make the clotted (scald) cream, pour milk into a large, heatproof bowl. Leave in a cool place overnight. The cream will rise to the surface. Place the bowl with milk in a stable pan with approx. 3 cm water and leave to simmer for two to three hours until the milk becomes solid. Leave to cool and scoop off the cream with a perforated spoon. Store in the fridge.

If this sounds like too much hard work, just buy some clotted cream from your local delicatessen or supermarket.

LOOE – AT THE WATER'S EDGE

THE TOWN OF LOOE, WHOSE NAME COULD BE CONFUSED WITH ANOTHER (PRIVY) PLACE, IS FOUND ON THE RIVER OF THE SAME NAME AND IS A FAMOUS FISHERS' METROPOLIS.

It is rare to get fish as fresh as in Looe. Fish auctioneer Julian (Simply Fish) tells us that the fish from here is sent to every corner of Great Britain, France and astonishingly also Los Angeles. Celebrity cook Gordon Ramsey gets his box of fresh fish daily from Looe. The fish here is so fresh because the fishermen and friends return to the home port daily to unload their fish. This is not the case everywhere. Many fishing boats stay at sea for days.

Next to numerous shops at the harbour such as the headquarters of the ice cream producer Treleavens, or the freshest fish and delicatessen at Pengelly's, there are also rows and rows of tourist and swimming equipment shops.

A TOWN OF TWO HALVES

Looe has two halves, one in the east and another in the west. The town is framed by idyllic, Cornish pastures, which at first

glance don't quite fit together with the fishing and sailing boats in the port. If you like, you can give the pastures a miss and go fishing. From mackerel to lobsters, you can catch everything here, it only depends on your equipment and distance to the coast. What's more, boats run from here (weather permitting) to Looe Island (also known as St George's Island). The slightly out-of-the-way island is a very wild and untouched nature reserve. Its story as a smugglers' den strangely came to an end when the main toll house was built here. Nowadays the island is managed by the Cornwall Wildlife Trust, who set a limit on the number of visitors.

SWIMMING IN LOOE

If you are looking for beaches and swimming opportunities, you are spoilt for choice in Looe. The small town has many to offer: Banjo Pier and Looe Beach turned the town into a swimming Mecca quite early on. Furthermore, the local Second Beach and Millendreath present opportunities to escape the crowds in case Banjo Pier and East Looe are too busy. Near the river is Hannafore Beach, one of the more peaceful beaches, which is great for a picnic with its grassy banks.

TIP: SHOPPING!

Pengelly's on the quay is perfect for fish and cooking enthusiasts. Here is everything a fish lover could ever need, including a good range of fresh sea creatures and diverse sauces, as well as spices that all fish cooks should have in their spice rack. Another option is to be at the fish market early in the morning (and this means 6:30 a.m.), if/when the fishers come back with their haul.

PENGELLY'S
THE QUAY, EAST LOOE, PL13 1DY
TEL. 01503 262246
WWW.PENGELLYS.CO.UK
(WITH A BRANCH IN LISKEARD)

FOOD LOVER

FRESH FISH MAKE FINE DISHES

EVERYDAY HARDWORKING FISHERMEN PULL FRESH FISH FROM THE ENGLISH CHANNEL AND IT MAKES GOURMETS SMILE. SCALLOPS, CRABS AND LOBSTERS – PURE POETRY!

LARSSON'S COFFEE HOUSE, LOOE

Martin Noble is an Englishman, who has spent some time on the Continent. In Bavaria (Germany) to be more exact. Then he came back to the UK and opened his colourful café in the middle of Looe. He called it 'Larsson's' in honour of the Swedish painter Carl Larsson. 'I wanted to serve real, good coffee here. And, of course some German specialities,' the funny guy tells us, in the odd German dialect they speak in Upper Franconia. The many Bavarian dishes from cheescake to bratwurst are worth a try. However, the one-of-a-kind Martin (complete with moustache!) actually specialises in crêpes, and they have funny names.

On special evenings (just enquire) Martin offers dining clubs between his four crazy walls featuring 'food from the Continent' and music evenings during which the café quickly transforms into a favourite meeting spot. All of this in the tiny town of Looe!

7 BULLER STREET,
EAST LOOE PL13 1AS
TEL. 01503 265368
WWW.LARSSONSCOFFEEHOUSE.COM

Martin in Larsson's

SAM'S ON THE BEACH, POLKERRIS

Any local will tell you to choose Sam's on the Beach when you visit one of the many Sam's in Fowey. The highly skilled team from Sam's have created something wonderful out of the former lifeboat house on Polkerris Beach. Where a lifeboat used to stand waiting to save lives (33 according to a notice board), there is now a sensational restaurant with a view of the ocean. Stone-baked pizzas with the thinnest crust, optionally with crab, the finest seafood and starters that will blow you out of the water satisfy a wide audience. If you're not a pizza lover, never fear – they also serve exceptional steaks and salads.

Outside, at a kind of ice cream kiosk, you can also buy take away pizzas, sandwiches or, of course, ice cream for the beach. In conclusion, Sam's on the Beach is a complete artwork for the taste buds.

14 POLKERRIS, PAR, PL24 2TL
TEL: 01726 812255
WWW.SAMSCORNWALL.CO.UK

BREAKFAST TIP:
BEACH BREAKFAST PIZZA WITH BACON, TOMATOES, MUSHROOMS, BAKED BEANS AND EGG.
LUNCH SANDWICHES FOR £6.

GOOD COP, BAD COP

GOOD COP: YUMMY, YUMMY IN MY TUMMY!

Cornwall and good food! They simply belong together. At first, you may not want to believe this fun fact, until you have sampled it for yourself. Just thinking about freshly caught fish, Cornish crab scattered over nachos or an original Cornish pizza makes your mouth start watering (in floods!). No matter which tavern your hungry legs take you to, you simply won't be disappointed by Cornwall. The fish & chips are crispy and delicious – you'll never find soggy chips here.

BAD COP: YOU DON'T HAVE TO TRY EVERYTHING!

Seriously, now: this Stargazy Pie! A dish where fish heads peer out of the pie crust, apparently gazing at the stars. Well, I see desperation in their eyes more than anything. Tradition may be tradition but you really don't have to try everything. You can even go wrong with the beloved pasty, by reaching for a thrown together, mass-produced one that will weigh on your stomach (heavily) for a very long time. So beware of 'traditional cuisine!'

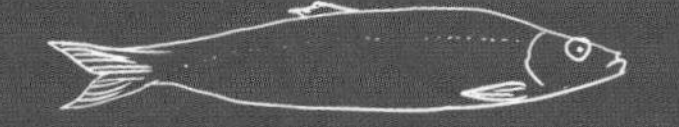

SHOPPING QUEEN

SLIGHTLY FRUITY

CIDER, APPLE JUICE OR GINGER BEER? IF YOU ARE LOOKING FOR THESE IN LARGE QUANTITIES, YOU CAN'T GO WRONG WITH CORNISH ORCHARDS' FARM SHOP…

Cornish Orchards did well to change their image. 'Since we've been working with the new labels, more people have been coming to try the cider and bottles are even being sent to Australia,' Sheila from the farm shop tells us. The bottles are lovely, with fruit trees on them, and they really invite you to take them home to your apartment, or to the next beach, and drink yourself merry. As well as the alcohol, there is of course the excellent apple juice (and we can judge this, because we come from Austria's number one apple region), lemonade and elderflower juice.

You can get a bit tipsy tasting the various cider products if you haven't eaten enough for breakfast or lunch. But this is good cider. Cornish Orchards not only offers something for those with a delicate palette (Farmhouse Cider), or a sweet tooth (Raspberry Blush Cider) but also for the hardy (Vintage Cider). So if Sheila can't convince you to buy something, you must be an avid beer drinker, and not a cider drinker.

CORNISH ORCHARDS
WESTNORTH MANOR FARM DULOE,
LISKEARD, PL14 4PW
TEL. 01503 269007
WWW.CORNISHORCHARDS.CO.UK

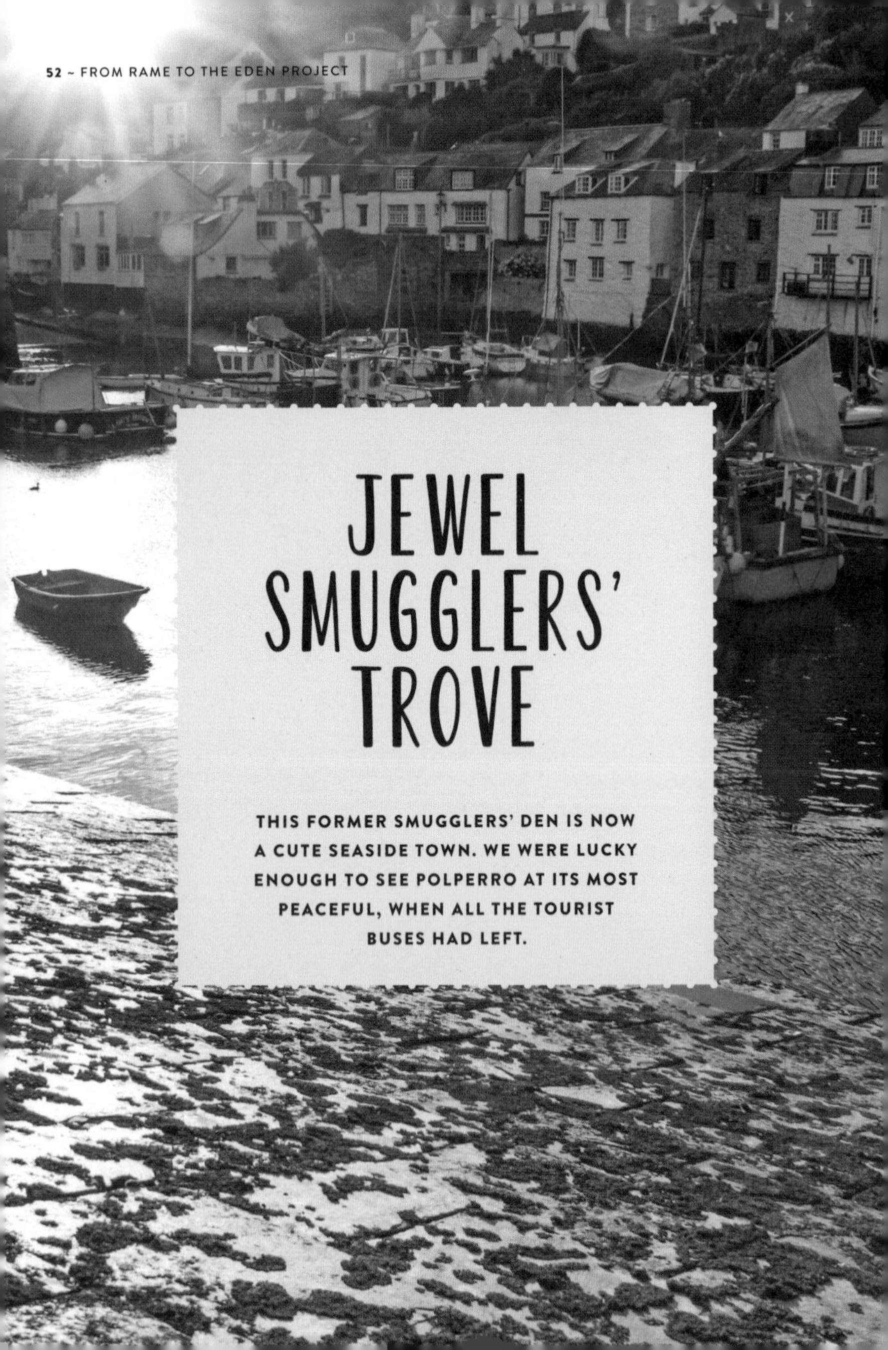

JEWEL SMUGGLERS' TROVE

THIS FORMER SMUGGLERS' DEN IS NOW A CUTE SEASIDE TOWN. WE WERE LUCKY ENOUGH TO SEE POLPERRO AT ITS MOST PEACEFUL, WHEN ALL THE TOURIST BUSES HAD LEFT.

When the car park is a few hundred metres away from the town centre in a place with approximately 1,000 inhabitants, my suspicion is aroused. It's true – it's a very popular town and you won't see it at its best at the height of the tourist season. However, if you wait until the end of the day, when all the tourist buses have gone home, you'll be able to experience all the delights of this jewel in the form of a smuggler's nest. We were fortunate that all of the buses had left for the day, so we only saw an amount of people proportionate to the number of inhabitants.

MR WILCOX

Anyone called Willy Wilcox must have been a sly old dog, which was true in this case: numerous legends surround the biggest smuggler in Polperro (who reputedly met his end in a cave on the small beach). Smuggling culture developed due to the English royal family imposing high taxation, on all manner of goods, for a long time. However in the nineteenth century there was no efficient regulatory body and thus two thirds of all tea drunk in England (and this was a lot, knowing the British) was smuggled goods. If you want to know more about Willy Wilcox, you can certainly chat about him with the locals over an ale or a cider in the 'best pub in the world', the Blue Peter.

ART & HISTORY

Judging by the the slanted walls in the alleys, it is apparent that Polperro is an ancient town. Partially whitewashed, partially natural stone, at sunset you don't need an overactive imagination to envisage how the town might have looked in the past. If you follow the signs to the Coast Path, you come to a beautiful viewing platform over the cliffs with a (more than) romantic bench. Although you can't watch the sunset here, you can gaze at the sea and lose yourself in the moment. If you visit Polperro during the day, you can take a look at the art collective's work. The town seems to not only have an incredibly inspiring appeal to visitors, but also to artists. Austrian artist Oskar Kokoschka didn't come here during the turmoil of the Second World War to continue painting for nothing.

TIP: HIKING

Hiking opportunities are always just around the corner in Cornwall. For instance, in Polperro you can go on a four to five hour hike to Looe and back.

You can swim in safe waters in the natural Chapel Pool, which by the way is only visible when the tide is in, and disappears to join the ocean when the tide goes out. The pool is found just a few metres outside the village centre. Many children from the town have learnt to swim in this pool, so it is probably a good job the sea cleans it out every so often!

BE THE CAPITAL JUST ONCE

LAUNCESTON AND LOSTWITHIEL BOTH HAVE EXPERIENCE OF BEING THE COUNTY TOWN OF CORNWALL. IN THE THIRTEENTH CENTURY THE TOWNS SWITCHED PLACES AND LOSTWITHIEL GRACEFULLY ACCEPTED THE HONOUR. TODAY TRURO IS THE CAPITAL AND THE TWO 'L' TOWNS HAVE TAKEN ON OTHER ROLES.

A walk through Launceston absolutely has to end in a coffee house or at a dining table. Be it at the café and deli №8, at Liberty Coffee with its adjoining brasserie or at Little Bakehouse, it is completely at your discretion. A detour to the Little Bakehouse led us to the soup of the day, but we wouldn't have said no to the sourdough toasts (with salmon and scrambled egg) or the sandwiches. A star of the town is the butcher, Philip Warren, who is a master of regional specialties.

LOSTWITHIEL

Lostwithiel is authentic – the Cornish love living here, and wandering up to Restormel Castle. Tourist traps are few on the ground; instead you'll find more of a predilection for tasteful antiques and well-visited food, cider and beer festivals. The narrow path often leads guests up to the Duchy of Cornwall to partake in a cream tea or to look for Prince Charles, to whom the estate belongs.

MUSEUM

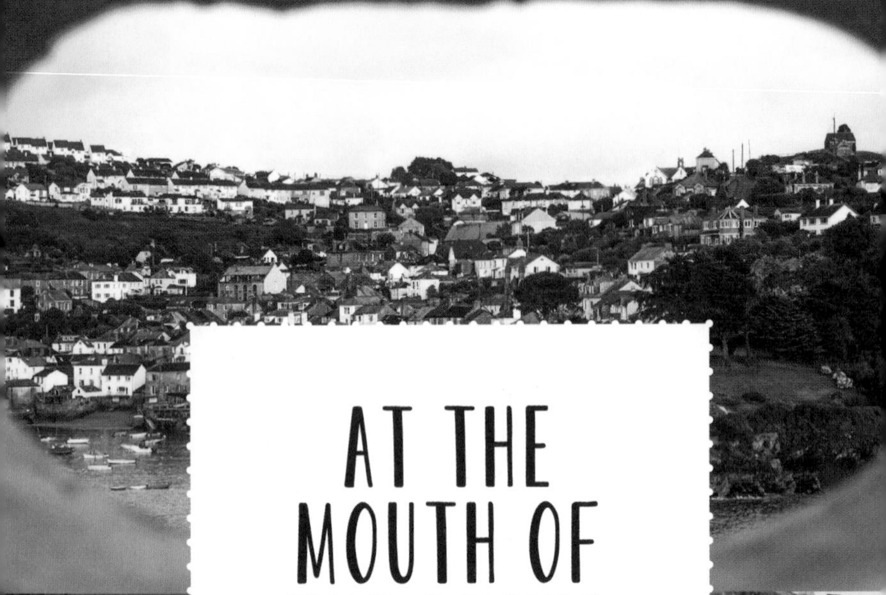

AT THE MOUTH OF THE RIVER

FOWEY (SAY: 'FOY') COULD PASS AS AN EASTERN ST IVES. THE ONLY DIFFERENCE BEING THAT PEOPLE KAYAK AND SAIL INSTEAD OF SURF.

Yeah, this is the true home of sailing. Fittingly, there are yacht clubs, sailmakers, water taxis, sailing schools and boat rentals. Aside from sailing, there are lots of possibilities for getting on the water: you can join a cruise, boats take you upstream to Lostwithiel, and there are also fishing boats that will gladly take you with them. Kitesurfers also like to get lost in the area and Par Sands, for example, offers good conditions for this activity. And then there are the many colourful kayaks and canoes that are waiting to be let loose in the water. Fowey is an ideal playground for both the experienced and inexperienced, and there are several stations where kayaks and canoes are ready to be rented. There are also guided tours for beginners.

If you would rather go to the countryside, there are a multitude of possibilities: hiking on the South West Coast Path or along the river Fowey, golfing in Lostwithiel or Lanhydrock, or walking along Saint's Way to Padstow. The many beaches in the area make it possible to not have to even enter the water. If you are looking for a holiday read, you should get hold of the author Daphne du Maurier's works. This novelist spent a great deal of time in Cornwall and Fowey and aptly, the places in her stories can be found here, if you go looking.

Worked up an appetite? Sam's in Fowey has more of an American than Cornish feel to it. There is Elvis and friends for the ears, and burgers and seafood for the belly. No matter how enamoured with America it may seem, local ingredients are an unconditional necessity. This makes Sam's a very popular place, and there are even a few branches now: in Truro, on Polkerris Beach or in the form of the Sam's Vans.

THIS AND THAT:

NEED A CHANGE OF PERSPECTIVE?
GO UP TO
ST CATHERINE'S CASTLE!

FOOD AND DRINK:
PINKY MURPHY'S

MORE INFORMATION ABOUT
THE PORT AND SAILING:
WWW.FOWEYHARBOUR.CO.UK

THINK TWICE

HOLIDAY WITH THE (W)RIGHT FAMILY

STONE BY STONE – THE WRIGHT FAMILY HAS BUILT A GOOD FAMILY VENTURE OVER THREE GENERATIONS AND FORTY YEARS. THE TIMES WHEN THE FAMILY HAD TO LIVE IN THE CAMPERVAN (DURING CONSTRUCTION WORKS) ARE OVER. TODAY 15 LOVINGLY FURNISHED COTTAGES GLEAM, EACH DELIGHTFUL IN ITS OWN UNIQUE WAY.

Holly Wright runs the Treworgey Estate together with her parents ('who just won't leave it alone and retire'). This is home to the 15 holiday cottages as well as a swimming pool, 21 horses and above all, the small, black Rabbit that is in fact a dog. (Actually, with her dark coat, Rabbit is more like Holly's shadow.) The cottages were furnished by Holly's mum Linda, who likes to drive to Lostwithiel and go antique shopping. 'These used to be old farmhouses,' says Holly, who still finds it odd that there are no straight walls. Despite the houses' dignified age, you will not want for anything in the five star accommodation. Quite the opposite: the cottages are so well-received, that they have even been awarded the official seal of Self Catering Holiday Provider of the Year. 'Hear, hear!'

Holly & Mum Linda

ECO IS YOUR FRIEND

Even in the 1970s it was possible to work sustainably. 'People used to look at my parents strangely because they were interested in special materials, solar panels and things like that,' says Holly about the early days. Today the trend is moving in a more environmentally friendly direction, thank goodness, but the family in Treworgey have been at it for a long time. And while we are pottering about the houses, it suddenly turns into pitch-black night time – a starry sky has drawn over the lovely, hilly landscape and the view to Looe disappears steadily into the distance. If we didn't already have another place booked, we would have preferred to stay here.

DULOE, LOOE, PL14 4PP

TEL. 01503 262730

WWW.CORNISHDREAMCOTTAGES.CO.UK

Dear diary...
a trip to the Eden Project is
always an experience and has
a different effect on everyone.
We recount our experiences here
energetically and realistically – as
it should be for the Eden Project.

THINK TWICE

Once you're at West Taphouse, it takes no time at all to get to the Eden Project. A project that is all about sustainability, nature and other environmental projects was perfectly suited to our book. We set off quite early in the morning, only to find that about 100 other people had the exact same idea. We parked at Lime 1 – here we can only advise other scatterbrained drivers like us, or those who would never admit to having no sense of orientation, to make sure you remember the fruit and number where you parked. The journey back to the car park is only possible by bus and it sticks rigidly to the fruity agenda. Caution, the bus stops at Plum, Pineapple, Lime and Melon but never at Apple or Orange. How could any normal person have figured this out?

GIANT HONEYCOMBS

You work up certain expectations for sights that you have been waiting to see for a long time. For example, I thought the Statue of Liberty was larger and the Golden Gate Bridge was smaller than I experienced them in reality. At the Eden Project it was exactly the same as with that blood-red Californian beauty: it was enormous! According to Lonely Planet, even the Tower of London can fit inside – they must have tried it. Here, in the middle of nowhere, near the mini town of Lostwithiel (this used to be the capital of Cornwall, see page 55), the largest greenhouses in the world were built from scratch. In an ugly kaolin pit, a project for nature was erected in no time at all. In the 20 minute film about the building of this monster project, founded by Tim Smit, you can see what pressure the builders were under. As it rained for no less than 100 days back-to-back(!) in the Cornish winter of 2000 to 2001, the construction was delayed quite a bit, so they had to work intensively, until the break of dawn on the official opening day.

HOT HOT HOT

Since March 2001 the Eden Project has permanently been on the map for many visitors, as a perfect rainy-day activity – we had a hefty downpour when we visited! The best climatic conditions for tropical and mediterranean environments were created in the two biomes. Now you can see cacti, silvery olive trees, palms and banana trees in close proximity. At first I was slightly sceptical when an amusing sign in the tropical greenhouse advised that I should go through jumperless and should definitely take water with me. 'Rubbish!' I thought, and did not bother to detach myself from my cosy jumper, which spelled my downfall only two minutes later. The humidity suddenly rose and the sun came through the honeycomb with a vengeance. Shortly before collapsing, I did remove my outermost layer of clothing and it was a good idea. In retrospect I would advise everyone to take the sign at its word and for half an hour, put aside the general advice in Cornwall of always wearing a cosy jumper.

COFFEE AND SCONES

Like all tourist attractions, the Eden Project has a tourist shop as well as a café, only they are refreshingly different. In the shop there are only fair-trade or recycled items, that are well-suited to conscientious souvenirs, and the café has its own sustainability rules. The gastronomical section is probably the most recent part of the entire complex: it used to be inundated with guests and had to be reborn like a phoenix rising from the ashes.

BODELVA,
NEAR ST AUSTELL, PL24 2SG
TEL. 01726 811911
WWW.EDENPROJECT.COM

Landtrain
this way

Game Rules
Eden Project Café

Help yourself to whatever you like.

You have to fill your drinks using the cups at the side. You can refill these as often as you like!

The focaccias are so big, you'll struggle to eat a whole one.

If you want a scone, then consider sharing it, or else you may not be hungry for the next two days.

Scones should be prepared as follows: butter, a dollop of jam and then as much clotted cream as is humanly possible! Done!

For tea and coffee simply queue up where you see the signs – this can take quite some time.

To pay, simply tell the cashier what you had.

I ♡ Shopping
SHOPPING QUEEN
IT'S ALWAYS
TEA OR COFFEE
O'CLOCK
TEL. 01503 264476
WWW.CORNISH-TEA.CO.UK
CORNISH COFFEE
CORNISH COFFEE
CORNISH COFFEE
CORNISH COFFEE
LET IT RIP!
WHO ARE WE?
GET IN TOUCH

CORNISH TEA AND COFFEE ARE DUNCAN AND TOM 'WITH A HELPING HAND FROM UNCLE HARVEY'. THESE TWO HAD A DREAM. THEY WANTED TO CREATE SOMETHING THAT EVERYONE COULD ENJOY AND THAT WOULD DO JUSTICE TO THEIR HOME, CORNWALL. THEN THE KETTLE WHISTLED, AND THEY JUST KNEW THAT THEY WOULD SPECIALISE IN CORNISH TEA.

In 2012 they created a tea called Smuggler's Brew, which was fit for everyday use. To find this perfect blend, there was one tea tasting after another. Duncan explains that they were simply looking for a tea that tastes good with milk and sugar, because 'that's how we drink tea here'.

The success is due to the carefully-selected blend. The orange and black packaging catches your eye, not only with its bright colouring, but also with its short story about 'local heroes' from Cornwall and around the world, making this brew quite an experience. Duncan's kids were featured on Smuggler's Brew, which still makes them proud today.

These restless Cornish entrepreneurs keep coming up with bright ideas for what they can put on their colourful packaging. Just recently they created coffee blends answering to the names of Italian Style and Stupidly Strong. On the website they harness this creative energy; there is an online calculator to find out how much tea or coffee you need in a year, so all of your tea and coffee needs are catered for year in, year out. On their love for the British hot drink they say:

'We love tea – You'll love our tea – We could all be happy together.'

Lisa and Tom

TRURO, FALMOUTH, ROSELAND & THE LIZARD

Every town should have a peninsula! This seems to be the topic of this chapter. A journey of discovery for puzzle lovers, shipwreck divers, cheese lovers, nature enthusiasts, pasty bakers, tea drinkers and culture lovers.

Helston
Penwith
Porthleven
LOE BAR
MULLION COVE
PREDANNACK HEAD
Cadgwith
LIZARD DOWNS
The Lizard
KYNANCE COVE

Helford

Manaccan

Roseland, Truro,
Falmouth,
Fowey, Looe, Rame

St. Keverne

THE
MANACLES

Coverack

BLACK
HEAD

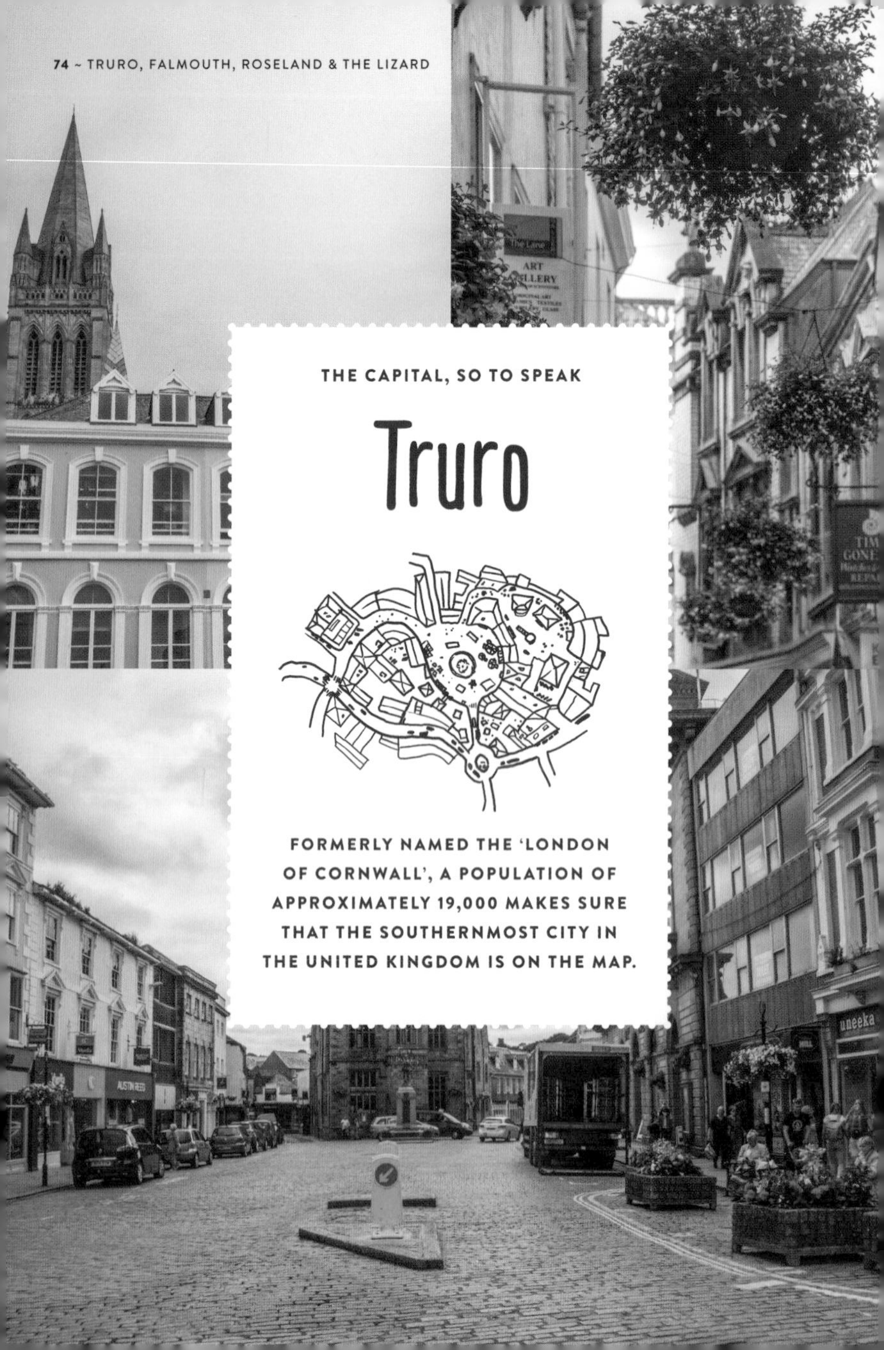

THE CAPITAL, SO TO SPEAK

Truro

FORMERLY NAMED THE 'LONDON OF CORNWALL', A POPULATION OF APPROXIMATELY 19,000 MAKES SURE THAT THE SOUTHERNMOST CITY IN THE UNITED KINGDOM IS ON THE MAP.

From the amount of traffic alone you can tell that Truro is more city than countryside. The roads are restless and there are a lot of shops and farmers' markets. Many companies and organisations are based here, however don't expect a capital city.

The Tourist Info is well-equipped and an ideal place to gather lots of information about Cornwall. For example, it offers a large selection of Treasure Trails: the widest range of treasure-hunting routes and puzzles for various places in Cornwall that you could wish for. Lemon Street Market is also worth a visit, with its petite and exquisite shops, including a gallery and café on the first floor.

It is worth popping round to Baker Tom's. If you are going self-catering in Cornwall, then the Cornish Food Box is a hot tip, or the Great Cornish Food Store. Don't hesitate to get a week's worth of local produce!

Want a bit of culture and entertainment? In Truro there is the Hall for Cornwall, a centre for theatre, concerts, musicals and more. Maybe there's something suitable here for you...?

TIP: THE OLD GRAMMAR SCHOOL AND THE BAKING BIRD (CAKES!)

If you want to escape the rain, a trip to Truro is definitely worth it. You can visit shops, drink tea/coffee, take a tour of Skinner's Brewery or venture to the bowling hall to strike a few bowling pins.

As Truro lies on a river, not next to the sea, you may as well leave your beach equipment at home. Instead, engage in some people-watching as the Cornish go about their everyday life. Truro is on the itinerary if you want to mingle with the crowd, or feel the need to treat yourself to some 'big city' bustle.

HERE IS A TRAVEL-GUIDE APPROPRIATE TIP: TRURO IS FAMOUS FOR ITS NEO-GOTHIC CATHEDRAL WHICH IS A DISTINCTIVE PART OF THE CITYSCAPE.

Cheese as an Art Form

Next to clotted cream and pasties, Yarg is another treat that will immediately make you think of the country's southernmost county. And it is produced near Truro. Yarg – actually 'gray' spelt backwards – is produced at Lynher Dairies Cheese Company, and is exported to the entire world. Once this semi-firm cheese has melted in your mouth, you'll want it again and again.

The special thing about this cow's milk cheese is that it is dressed in stinging nettles, which lose their sting when consumed.

SOMETIMES NETTLE, SOMETIMES GARLIC

Sometimes the nettles change for a suit of wild Cornish garlic. If you are in Cornwall, you should pop round to the farm near Truro for a piece of cheese, or any cheese shop in the region and discover it. It doesn't just go well with bread, it is also excellent to cook with. The best partner a Cornish Yarg could have will always be the tomato. Have fun with this flavourful fusion. Even if you become addicted to Yarg afterwards, there is help, as Catherine from Lynher Dairies confirms: 'We will send our cheeses gladly to any country! Just order on our homepage and have a bit of patience, then you can enjoy it.'

WWW.LYNHERDAIRIES.CO.UK

Say Cheese!

Catherine from Lynher Dairies

What is special about your dairy?

That everything is produced by hand and we have kept our personnel over the years. Compared to many competitors, we are very small. The Cornish nettles we collect in May and June give the Yarg its distinctive flavour. It reminds a lot of people of mushrooms. Yarg is as traditional as the pasty in Cornwall.

Where is your favourite place to eat your pasties?

On the beach, preferably at Kynance Cove. It's just so dramatically beautiful.

What was your first impression of Cornwall and what has changed since then?

I came here for the first time 30 years ago. It used to be a lot quieter and more rural. Since I'm from London, the peace and quiet was a welcome change for me. Cornwall used to be a popular place to retire and so there were lots of elderly people here. This has changed a bit since then: today there are a lot of young people who have chosen to live here.

What do you appreciate about Cornish culture?

That a lot of creativity has appeared. From the artists in St Ives, to the theatre group Kneehigh, to the musicians in Penzance.

CATHERINE'S TIPS:

PORTHMEOR CAFÉ IN ST IVES

TRELOWARREN/NEW YARD (COTTAGES AND RESTAURANT NEAR HELSTON), TEL. 01326 22 15 95 WWW.TRELOWARREN.COM

Both have good, local food!

A LAND BEFORE OUR TIME

Roseland

PENINSULA

Despite all expectations, the name Roseland probably does not come from the lush vegetation of this magical place but from the Cornish Rosinis for moor island – we still believe the first explanation because the peninsula is so beautiful.

Time seems to have stood still on the Roseland Peninsula. The King Harry Ferry has been coming here from the Falmouth area over the river Fal for nearly 100 years. We chose the path from Truro, by the way – there's something beautiful about making your way slowly to St Mawes. We made a note to rent one of the comfy cottages here, next time we come to Cornwall. It would be wonderful to discover this region with plenty of time on your hands. We came with the Treasure Trails in mind, because we are keen puzzle fans, and you get to see a lot of Roseland on the suggested path for the *Roseland Murder Mystery Trails.*

NATURAL BEAUTY

Roseland really is a natural beauty. Tropical plants as far as the eye can see, and usually framed by a view of the ocean or – in this case even better – the view of the river in front of the St Just in Roseland Church. This was, without doubt, one of the most beautiful places that we have ever seen. In front of the car park you walk through the ancient graveyard following the direction of the church. Above you, giant treetops sit enthroned, inhabited by flocks of birds making mystical sounds. When you arrive at the church, which by the way is also surrounded by palms, an expanse of water opens up in front of you.

LOOKING PROMISING

At St Anthony Head you are blessed with a vision. Here is a perfect view of the mouth of the Fal River, all the way up to Falmouth. There's an old military station which can in fact be rented, as the National Trust has turned the little houses into apartments. You can enjoy a good book and a glass of wine, complete with a view of the sea from the small terrace. There are worse ways to spend your time. If you have a moment, it's a good idea to hike up the South West Coast Path.

SIMPLY CHARMING

The villages and towns are called Portscatho, Portloe, Veryan and St Mawes, and they are all captivating. Veryan oozes charm even without being next to the ocean and has a beautiful, public lake, right next to the church. Otherwise you can find fishing villages right out of books or – in the case of Portloe – right out of films. In St Mawes you can reward yourself after an eventful Roseland-day at a local pub:

THE RISING SUN
TR2 5DJ, TEL. 01326 27 02 33
&
THE VICTORY INN
TR2 5DQ, TEL. 01326 270324
ON A SMALL SIDE STREET

~

OR WITHOUT PUB GRUB –
THE IDLE ROCKS
HARBOURSIDE, ST MAWES
TEL. 01326 270270
WWW.IDLEROCKS.COM

SHOPPING QUEEN

The Somewhat Different Tea Plantation

TEA PLANTS ARE FOUND LARGELY IN (FORMER) ENGLISH COLONIES. YET NEAR TRURO, A MIRACLE HAS TAKEN PLACE, AND IT IS CALLED TREGOTHNAN.

You could attribute it to the Gulf Stream, the Cornish sun or the laid back character of the Cornish, but there is a tea plantation in Cornwall. The home of the Boscawen family (since 1335) is today the only tea producer in England that also grows on home soil. You can get a closer look during a visit, though you do need to make a request online at least one day in advance. They really do work here, so as a visitor, the best place to go is the small tea shop. It is a wonder to behold with its magnificent, colourful packages of tea.

BEST TIME TO VISIT: ANNUAL CHARITY GARDEN OPEN WEEKEND (IN SPRING, DATE CHANGES EVERY YEAR!)

~

SHOP ADDRESS:
TRESILLIAN, TRURO, TR2 4AJ
TEL. 01872 520000
WWW.TREGOTHNAN.CO.UK

SHOPPING QUEEN

It's Falmouth Time!

'THE TOWN ON THE RIVER FAL IS AN EXCELLENT STARTING POINT FOR ALL POSSIBLE EXCURSIONS,' THINKS THE SIGHTSEER OF TODAY. THE LOCALS ALSO USED TO THINK THIS. SOUVENIRS, PLANTS AND THE LIKE WERE NOT SHIPPED IN THROUGH THIS TOWN'S NATURAL PORT FOR NOTHING.

Tourism has given Falmouth a rebirth, following the collapse of its seafaring fortunes during the twentieth century. The deepest port in western Europe made Falmouth predestined for docking. This is how the greatest parcel station of the empire was created: for 150 years, nothing was sent to or from England without it going through Falmouth. Today visitors are mainly washed up – but this is entirely bearable in this student town that has dolled up a lot in the past few years.

MINGLE

You will always get a table in Falmouth and the roads are not as crammed as some places, the Adriatic coast for example. Combining the word 'gentle' with tourism brings with it a few advantages. It is possible to mingle with the locals, get involved in conversations or simply experience an entire holiday without the hustle and bustle.

CHURCH STREET

Even parting with your cash doesn't seem so bad when there's bunting to cheer you up. The best thing to do is grab an ice cream at Roskilly's while walking from the Joules window display to Fatface. You could take longer over some real highlights like Willow & Stone, which actually specialises in doorknobs, but also stocks antiques and stationery. You'll discover what you are looking for in Beerwolf Books, even if you later change your mind: books, beer, table football and every other kind of cult distraction all come together under one roof here. It is possible that you will be unable to tear yourself away from this shop. Other alternatives include the Hand Bar, which has something for absolutely everyone with more than 70 different types of beer. Pure liquid happiness! And once you've worked up an appetite, we highly recommend giving the best burger in Falmouth a try: The Meat Counter offers, amongst other classics, the Notorious B I G burger, which contains no less than two x beef patties and four x slices of cheese. There's always room for a coffee afterwards too. Head to Espressini for the best one.

STARTING POINT

Next to shopping in Falmouth, studying at the university or visiting museums (National Maritime Museum Cornwall) are quite superb. The town is perfectly located as a starting point for less lively places, such as the Roseland Peninsula or the Lizard Peninsula. There you can follow the South West Coast Path, or simply potter from one delightful village to the next.

TOWN-SEA-RIVER

'On the River Fal we are captains'. It doesn't matter whether you are hoisting the sails, taking a kayak paddle in your hand, or zipping around on motorboats, the River Fal is fun and attracts many locals, along with ordinary tourists and even Hollywood stars. In the enchanted, overgrown bays of the river, *Treasure Island* and other films have been shot, moreover, Pierce Brosnan apparently lives around here in a green house – well-camouflaged in the middle of southwest England's lush pastures. When visiting, the authors of this book (aka: us!) did not manage to run into Brad Pitt, but he was here shooting a film – we swear!

TIPS:

~

THE WHEELHOUSE:
REALLY GOOD SEAFOOD –
BOOK IN ADVANCE!
UPTON SLIP, FALMOUTH, TR11 3DQ
TEL. 0326 318050

~

THE GYLLYNGDUNE GARDENS

THINK TWICE

Natural Big Player

THE NATIONAL TRUST COULD BOAST ABOUT BEING THE LARGEST NATURE CONSERVATION ORGANISATION IN EUROPE. YET IT DOESN'T, IT JUST DOES ITS JOB: IN ENGLAND, NORTHERN IRELAND AND WALES, INSPECTING AND PROTECTING, PRESERVING AND RENOVATING.

A multitude of houses, industrial buildings, churches and chapels are in the care of the National Trust. This umbrella organisation, founded in 1895, makes sure that historical houses and gardens or valuable wood, beach and moor areas remain protected. More than 4.1 million members support them in doing this. The benefits? They can get into all properties and park in all National Trust car parks for free. For an individual membership it costs £64.80 a year, and where the National Trust is committed and well respected, people have no qualms spending this amount of money. (Their crazily large number of members does not come from nothing!) Of course there are also many National Trust buildings and areas in Cornwall, last but not least the coastal area. Hundreds of miles of coastline around the country are maintained by the National Trust, 10 per cent of the entire coastline in fact. Self-catering accommodation as well as B&Bs and hotels have been been created from the many historical buildings. If you are looking for a very alternative holiday, you can look under the section Working Holidays on the homepage. It is actually possible to work helping out the National Trust for a certain time, getting to know a new (working) world.

TIP:

MEMBERSHIP FOR NON-UK VISITORS IS CALLED THE TOURIST PASS AND CAN BE BOUGHT FOR SEVEN OR 14 DAYS ON WWW.NATIONAL-TRUST.ORG
HOW MUCH? FROM £24

SEA VIEW

The Lizard Peninsula

A JEWEL IN THE SOUTH WEST, WITH ADORABLE VILLAGES, SUMPTUOUS PASTIES AND ASTOUNDINGLY WILD, SANDY BEACHES: THE LIZARD PENINSULA PROMISES A LOT AND DELIVERS EVEN MORE.

However, the Lizard Peninsula used to be feared: it used to be a thorn in the sides of many captains (or maybe in the sides of their boats?). But the shallow waters and dangerously craggy cliffs also have their positive sides. On the one hand, they look damned impressive. From around the southernmost point of England (Lizard Point) as well as from around Kynance Cove, they are an impressive sight. Hiking around the local stretches of the South West Coast Path is a must for avid walkers and is a treat for photographers. With luck, if you use a telescopic lense, you can even catch sight of marine animals. On the other hand, shipwreck divers totally get their money's worth. So if you have a diving licence and thick skin, you can – literally – go on a treasure hunt here. There are definitely people who have dreamt of doing this – including us, but don't get your hopes up! Historically, the Cornish used to be mainly fishers and miners, and money was tight, so if a well-stocked ship met its watery demise on their coast, everything that was not nailed down was taken. In conclusion: you'll find lots of shipwrecks, but probably not much treasure.

SWEET OVERLOAD

The Lizard Peninsula is like its people: rugged on the outside, lovely on the inside. Whilst the cliffs were cunningly trying to scratch the boats, small settlements such as St Keverne, Helford, Manaccan, or even Cadgwith really bring the typical picturesque landscape of Cornwall to life. Here in Helford for example, we are talking about thatched cottages, the loveliest house signs and flowers in abundance. A child has collected shells and is selling them for pennies, two ladies in front of the cottage are sharing the latest gossip. So, basically real English village life. Although, St Keverne and Cadgwith come across as a bit more authentic. In Manaccan we can recommend the very humorous, but still stylish, South Café (Church Lane, TR12 6HR, Tel. 01326 23 13 31). In Cadgwith

it is best to go to Cadgwith Cove Inn, as the locals do, or buy a fish at Jonathan's to cook yourself. It is super local, by the way, to buy a pub drink in a plastic cup and sit and watch the fishing boats in the sun. For the entire Cadgwith experience you can also rent a bedroom at the pub.

IT DOESN'T GET MORE SOUTHERN

If you want to take a gander at the tip of England, then it's better to see the southernmost, rather than the westernmost point. Lizard Point is much more peaceful and has a more beautiful lighthouse, plus a cheaper car park. The cliffs are at least as impressive as those from Land's End. Just around the corner – and in the area of The Lizard itself – the nice, relatively new café and restaurant Coast Coffee Bar & Bistro will take care of all of your food and beverage needs after a long hike. A very popular choice is Ann's Pasties. Apparently the best far and wide. Accommodation is best found in one of the many B&Bs in Helston, as it is a slightly larger town, and is also a good starting point for all kinds of Cornwall activities.

TIP FOR THE BRAVE SHIPWRECK DIVERS:

AT DIVE FALMOUTH YOU CAN FIND OUT ABOUT ANYTHING AND EVERYTHING (SHIPWRECK) DIVING IN CORNWALL: WWW.DIVEFALMOUTH.CO.UK

FOOD LOVER

Roskilly's

LOTS AND LOTS OF COLOURFUL COWS. THE TRADEMARK OF THIS ICE CREAM FROM LIZARD.

Wherever you look in Cornwall, the colourful signs of Roskilly's Ice Cream shine back at you. This organic eatery has managed the leap into nearly every shop in the county, and enjoys great popularity. You can also visit Roskilly's Farm to look behind the scenes, buy Cornish products or to feast at Croust House.

Tregellast Barton Farm (aka Roskilly's Farm) is appreciated by the young and old, is easy to access with a pram or wheelchair and entry is free. You can walk on lush pastures, become acquainted with the everyday life of the farm, watch cows being milked and, of course, try the various different types of ice cream and fudges. If you get addicted to Roskilly's, you can find new supplies all across Cornwall.

TIP:

After feasting, go surfing at Kennack Sands (15 min), Pentreath (30 min) or Porthleven (30 min) for example – not really for beginners though.

ROSKILLY'S
ICE CREAM & ORGANIC FARM
TREGELLAST BARTON, ST KEVERNE
HELSTON, TR12 6NX
TEL. 01326 280479
WWW.ROSKILLYS.CO.UK

Treasure Trails

Interview with Tom from Treasure Trails

The first Treasure Trail was for Polperro. There were many to follow after that, and Great Britain is now dotted with entertaining and exciting trails, with the most diverse topics.

HOW LONG HAVE TREASURE TRAILS EXISTED?

It all started in 2005. Steve the founder invented a Treasure Trail for a charity event.

Tom

This murder mystery was so popular that Steve immediately wrote a few others. It was never intended to develop into a business model.

HOW MANY TREASURE TRAILS ARE THERE NOW?

At the moment there are over 1,000 Treasure Trails, spread across the entire United Kingdom. Not all of them are in Cornwall and not all of them are by Steve. There are also franchises which add to the opportunities.

WHAT'S YOUR LATEST TRICK?

There is now a Poldark Puzzle – amazing for all fans of the BBC series.

WARNING! TREASURE TRAILS CAN BE ADDICTIVE.

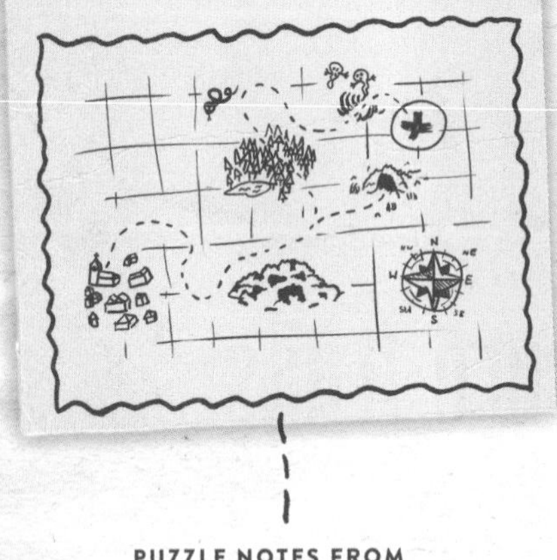

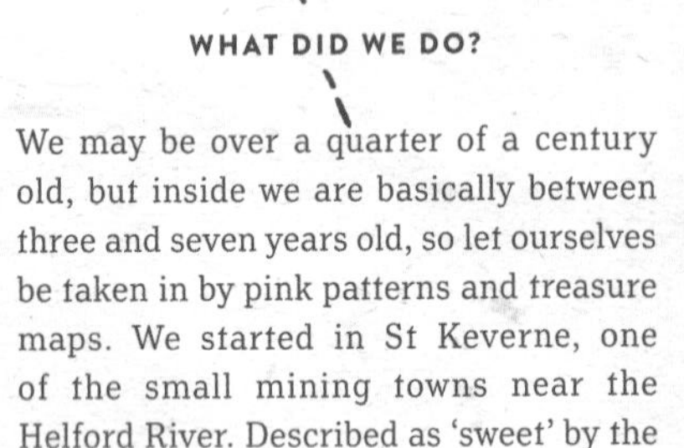

PUZZLE NOTES FROM TWO RIDDLE-SOLVERS

The meeting up of Eat Surf Live and Treasure Trails allowed our boldest childhood dreams to become reality. Discovered almost by chance, at the Tourist Information Office of Truro, little Katharina and little Vera couldn't resist it and scraped a few pounds together to snap one up in A5 format. Helford was planned for the next day.

WHAT DID WE DO?

We may be over a quarter of a century old, but inside we are basically between three and seven years old, so let ourselves be taken in by pink patterns and treasure maps. We started in St Keverne, one of the small mining towns near the Helford River. Described as 'sweet' by the locals, we were reassured. And it was. It really was!

THE SLIGHTLY DIFFERENT 'GUIDE'

We got to know our new guide better very quickly; it had so-called 'clues' at the ready for us, as well as directions. The clue always has something to do with the place where you are at the time and was – despite having studied English (ahem) – still quite hard to solve. When we found the solution, we were able to cross out the name we had uncovered, on the reverse side of our travel guide, then slowly but surely we carried on.

Clue Example:
'To answer the clue there is no need to find.
What has been taken – just what's left behind.'

And? Not so easy, huh?

DEAR ST KEVERNE!

Apart from the tremendous adventure that brought back memories of all the treasure hunts we had ever been on, we encountered places that we would marry at the drop of a hat. Next to St Keverne, with its adorable main square and two hotels (White Hart and Three Tuns), the church and the surrounding area is especially worth seeing.

... the Next Hint

We were able to explore this considerably as we got lost exactly five times at Direction 05, then two hours, two apples, 12 sweat outbreaks, a downpour and 34 confused sheep later, we finally arrived at the destination – the Methodist Church. The paths were partly overgrown, partly clear, with a grandiose view of the sea. In just 15 minutes we met sheep, cows, horses, dogs and cats, but not a single person – a dream!

IT CONTINUES...

... to Manaccan. Even more lovely. Even more ideal and equipped with an ultracool café, where guests bustle around outside, even on the not so clear summer days: the South Café. Here came the second wave of hunger, which we fought off successfully with Cheddar crisps.

And when we had solved all of the puzzles in this area, the treasure map led us further on to Helford, a place the like of which we had never seen before. Our eyeballs nearly popped out at the sight of this sleepy village, with cute house names such as Christmas Cottage or Wednesday Cottage, emerging in front of us. Thatched roofs, whitewashed walls and a sea of flowers in front of every single house – the Cornwall of our dreams.

AND THE SOLUTION IS???

We are certainly not going to tell you that (you curious cucumber!), because we don't even know ourselves and thus we're not in possession of the answer. Not even the friendly waitress at the Down by the Riverside Café could put us out of our misery. So now you have a mission: come to Helford, solve the puzzle and share the solution with us, we will worship you all of our lives – at least!

Now we just need one more clue...

... yeah! Found it!

TIP – EATABLES

The Cornish Pasty

WRITING A BOOK ABOUT CORNWALL WITHOUT EVEN MENTIONING THESE NUTRITIOUS, FILLED BAKED PASTRIES? IMPOSSIBLE! CHRISTINE AND SHARON LEGGE GAVE US THEIR FAMILY RECIPE. YOU CAN ACTUALLY ORDER EXCELLENT PASTIES FROM THEM (FROZEN OR READY TO EAT).

INGREDIENTS FOR THE DOUGH:

*

450 G WHITE FLOUR
125 G BUTTER
125 G LARD/FAT
240 ML WATER
1 TABLESPOON SALT

INGREDIENTS FOR THE FILLING:

*

50 G TURNIPS
50 G ONIONS
90 G BEEF
90 G POTATOES
SALT AND PEPPER

DOUGH:

PASTY:

1 Put flour and salt in a bowl. Add butter and lard and mix slightly. Add the cold water and form all ingredients into a dough. Put the dough in the fridge whilst you prepare the filling.

Tip: Make the dough a day before!

2 Peel the turnips and onions and cut into small pieces. Peel the potatoes and grate them into thin slices (2×1 cm). Cut the beef into small pieces as well.

mmmm!

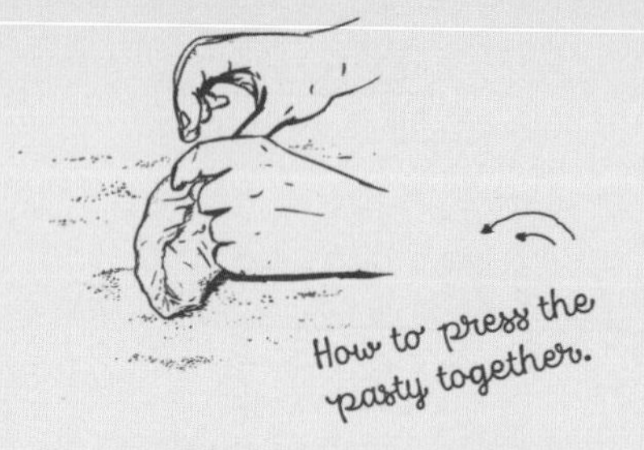

3 Roll out the pastry and cut into a circle, using a pot lid for example (diameter approximately 20 cm). Spread the majority of the turnips and onions on the pastry (leave some left over for the top layer of the filling). Then add the meat and season with salt and pepper. Now lay the potato slices on top and lightly salt some more. Use the rest of the turnips and onions for the top layer.

4 Pick up the dough at both ends and with the ingredients in the middle, fold in and press. Start pressing in the famous crust at one end, alternating between pressing in and folding the crust until you have reached the other end.

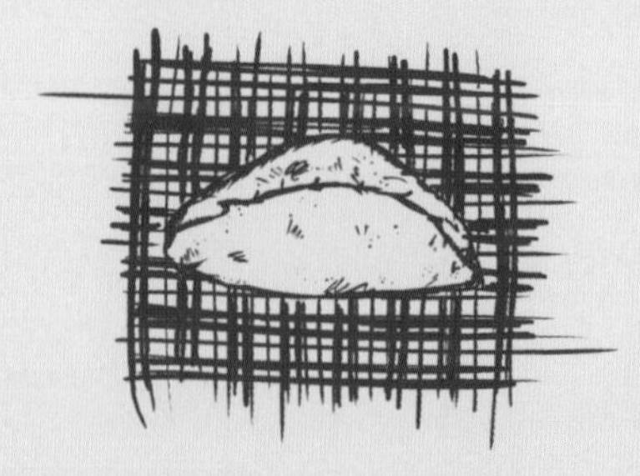

5 Pre-heat the oven to 180°C (Gas mark 4) and bake for an hour.

That's how we make a Leggy's Pasty!

LEGGY'S PASTIES
TEL. 01326 290683
RUAN MINOR, CORNWALL

PICTURE PERFECT

If you want to photograph the real Cornwall, then take your camera on a walk to the small fishing village of Cadgwith. To get there, make sure you do not miss the small sign on the main road, heading south. Once you are there, you walk through alleyways with white houses, thatched roofs, and meet cats, dogs, fishers and their boats. Most of the time a tractor can be found on the beach. It is used to pull fishing boats out of the water. If you walk north, a little up the South West Coast Path, you have a beautiful view of the entire village. The ascent is really worth it: you can sit a while on the wooden benches and watch the bustle of the thoroughly authentic village, and of course take photographs.

KYNANCE COVE

There are few places that can rock in any weather, but Kynance Cove is one of them (maybe because there are so many rocks here?). Just after the car park, at the lowest point of the Lizard Peninsula, you can enjoy a breathtaking view of the beach and the coastline. Good shoes are an advantage when you climb down the coast path, towards the beach. At the bottom there are a lot of people if the weather is good, and if it is pelting down with rain you could have this natural wonder all to yourself. For emergencies of all kinds (hunger, loo, etc.) there is also a café, however you will probably get more out of a picnic in the sand (although be careful, or else you might find yourself eating a SANDwich). If you visit Kynance Cove, you can assume you will get wet even without entering the water, as the breaking waves here are so powerful, even in good weather it constantly drizzles water droplets on the sandy beach. At Kynance Cove – for many locals the most beautiful beach in Cornwall, by the way – there are many caves to be discovered. All of them have funny names, such as the Kitchen, the Drawing Room or the Devil's Mouth. If you want to mingle with the merry folk and throw yourself into the water armed with a bodyboard or 'only' a wetsuit, you should always bear in mind that there is a strong current, so you should be careful!

SHOPPING QUEEN

Attention coffee drinkers!

MANY CAFÉS AND RESTAURANTS HAVE PUT THEIR MONEY ON ONE ROASTERY: ORIGIN. SO IF YOU SEE 'ORIGIN COFFEE IS SERVED HERE' AT THE ENTRANCE, THEN YOU KNOW THAT YOU CAN GET ITALIAN-QUALITY COFFEE.

Tom Sobey

Who do we have to thank for this? Bow down to... drum roll... Tom Sobey! Very early, at the tender age of eight years old, he came into contact with coffee through his parents' business. Having succumbed to the aroma, at 26 he founded a coffee roastery near Helston.

GOOD CONNECTION WITH COFFEE GROWERS

In the meantime he has accrued 40 members of staff, and very good contacts with coffee plantations, both in South America and worldwide. 'We manage a lot through the organisation "Fair Trade", but we also do a lot ourselves directly. Then our partners produce beans for us and are well rewarded,' he explains. 'But without the support of individual cafés in Cornwall, we wouldn't have been able to develop into what we are today.' Always with a smile on his lips and a charming, blue-eyed gaze, he shows us the sacks of coffee and the heart of

the business in Helston: the almost climate neutral roasting machines, which were 'not cheap'. After we had decided that we would also like to work in this atmosphere, with this coffee in our veins, Tom's colleague drops the boss' real title: 'he's the Rick Stein of coffee'. It'\s not only us who have to admit he's right, the restaurants Fifteen, Porthmeor as well as the Eden Project, and Rick Stein himself, did so too.

ORIGIN COFFEE AND EQUIPMENT ORDERS: WWW.ORIGINCOFFEE.CO.UK

~

A REAL ORIGIN COFFEEHOUSE IS NOW IN THE BEAUTIFUL TOWN OF PORTHLEVEN: A HOT TIP!

~

ORIGIN ALSO OFFERS COURSES: PERHAPS A GOOD PLAN FOR RAINY DAYS?

THE ROASTERY:
WHEAL VROSE BUSINESS PARK
HELSTON, TR13 0FG
TEL. 01326 574337
INFO@ORIGINCOFFEE.CO.UK

Many came to stay...

PENWITH PENINSULA

Famous surfer beaches, the magical St Michael's Mount, the town of Penzance and the historical mines define life on this peninsula. The old, the authentic and the newly arrived make this place endearing and unforgettable.

PENDEEN WATCH

St. Ives

Pendeen

CAPE CORNWALL

St. Just

SENNEN COVE

LAND's END

Sennen

Porthcurno

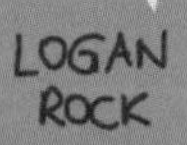

LOGAN ROCK

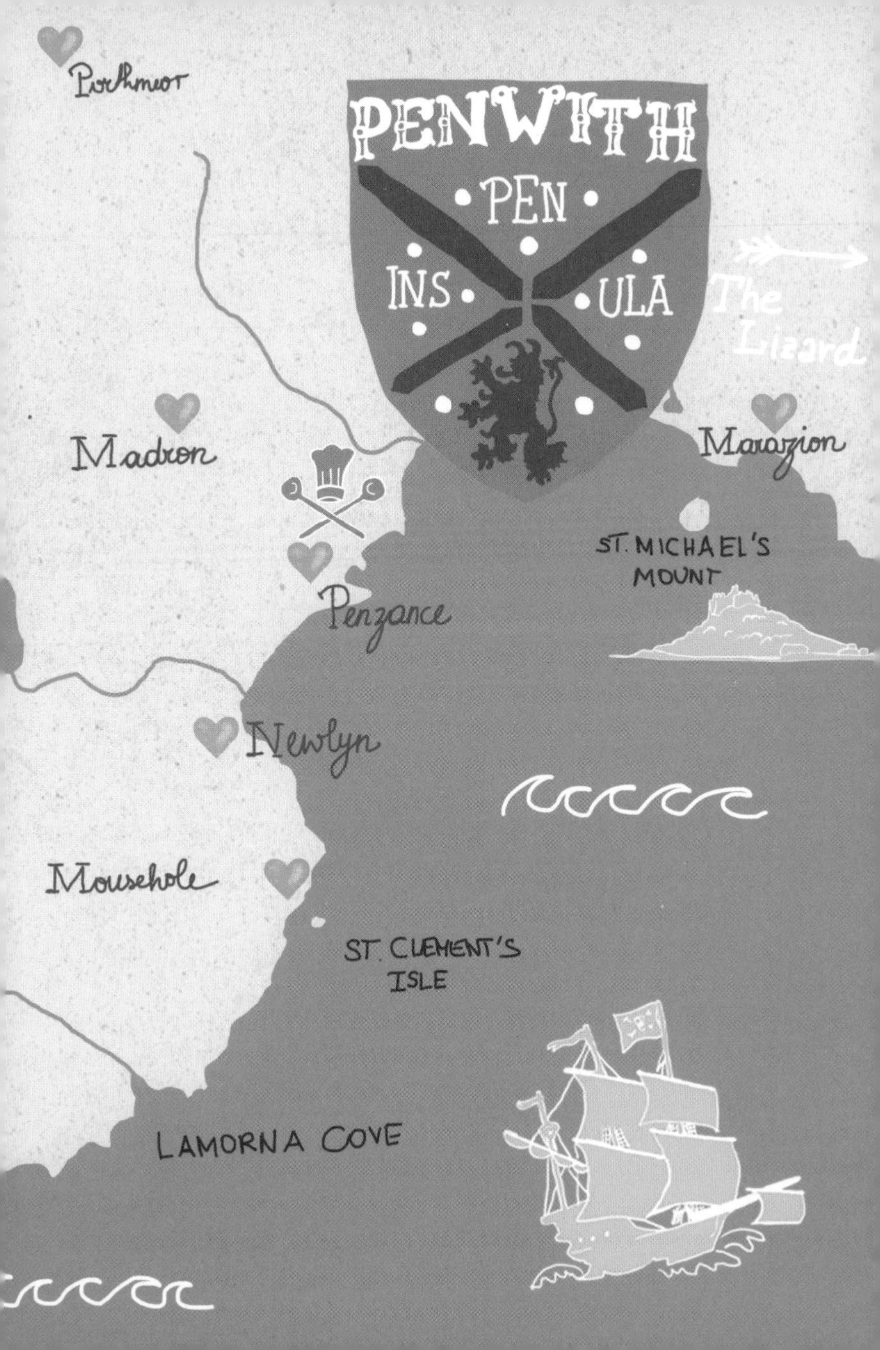
Porthmeor
PENWITH
PEN
INS
ULA
The Lizard
Madron
Marazion
ST. MICHAEL'S MOUNT
Penzance
Newlyn
Mousehole
ST. CLEMENT'S ISLE
LAMORNA COVE

SENSE THE MAGIC AND CHARM OF THE TOWN NEXT TO ST MICHAEL'S MOUNT.

MARAZION

Five minutes away from Penzance by car, 15 minutes by bus and probably 65 walking, the small town of Marazion is especially known for St Michael's Mount. Easy to espy from all corners of Marazion, this former pilgrimage point gives the town a particular flair. If you want to get there, you can go by boat or, when the tide is out, walk to this tidal island which is home to a former monastery/fort with its rock garden. Some Cornish believe that powerful ley lines meet here, which cause people to feel particularly attracted to this place. If you don't feel like climbing, or if you're not strapped up with your pilgrim's rucksack, come to windsurf in Marazion. Or just let yourself be charmed and spoilt by the relaxed Ben's Cornish Kitchen or the friendly Café Delicious. If you don't want to be indoors, then take a ready-made picnic basket from Delicious with you, to the beach or for a walk.

TIP: GO BY BIKE TO PENZANCE OR WALK THE 12.5 MILES TO ST IVES/LELANT ON ST MICHAEL'S WAY (THIS IS PART OF THE WAY OF ST JAMES, A PILGRIMAGE PATH).

Meet Orange Trevillion from Mount Haven Hotel

SHE DISCOVERED HER ENGLISH HAVEN FOR HERSELF: CORNWALL IS ORANGE'S JEWEL AMONGST THE COUNTIES.

What's special about Cornwall?

It's just a seductive place that you can't compare to any other. St Michael's Mount has a particular radiance to it. Four ley lines meet here, so this island has a very special energy that a lot of people can sense.

How did Mount Haven come about?

We came on holiday to this hotel for so many years, that we just ended up buying it. Then the hotel was renovated, and now you can see St Michael's Mount from everywhere, that was very important to me.

Did you already have experience in catering/hotels?

None at all. I was in advertising. But we always came to this hotel, which was already a coaching inn in 1840. Of course it looked a lot different then. The restaurant was full of armour, weapons and coats of arms and it was terribly haunted.

Ghosts... are there any left in Mount Haven?

No, we got rid of all of the ghosts. Something just lingers in a house where people always come and go. Everything should be OK now.

What role does surfing play in your life?

My son has his own surfing school, and opened a surfing camp in Morocco. We went surfing a lot in southwest France, because it was also my husband's hobby. Our entire life is centred around surfing.

ORANGE'S TIPS:

RESTAURANT: KOTA (PORTHLEVEN)

ST MICHAEL'S MOUNT & THE COAST BETWEEN LAMORNA AND LAND'S END (THERE ARE BEACHES, DOLPHINS, SEA LIONS...)

WITH A VIEW
OF THE HOLY MOUNTAIN:

MOUNT HAVEN HOTEL

When you arrive at the summit as we did, totally exhausted from a long trek from midtown Marazion, you are at first overwhelmed by the most beautiful view to be had for miles. The blue ocean, the grey St Michael's Mount and the faintest view of the town Penzance in the background make for really wonderful scenery for the hotel. Yet Mount Haven itself could actually manage that alone, with its baby blue and white rooms, which are so tastefully furnished. Hand in hand with a large balcony, it cannot easily be beaten. Whilst you're here, you should definitely make use of the other services: be it the incredible scones for cream tea on the terrace – with a view of St Michael's (we know), or the dinner that delights the palate. But watch out: if you try the latter, you may well not want to eat anywhere else, as the bread is so good, the butter so salty, the wine at its ideal temperature, the meat so perfect, the vegetables so fresh and the dessert so sweet.

MARAZION, PENZANCE, TR17 0DQ
TEL. 01736 719937
WWW.MOUNTHAVEN.CO.UK

HEN DELICATESSEN THE LO
illy
HUNTER&WALSH
HISTORIC CHAPEL STREET

A TOWN FOR THE CORNISH:

PENZANCE

MANY SAY THAT IT IS VERY CORNISH HERE. A PLACE TO READ A NEWSPAPER IN A CAFÉ ALONGSIDE THE LOCALS. A PLACE TO SWAY AT CONCERTS AND – FOR MANY – A PLACE TO STAY.

Penzance is the last stop on the train line from London to Cornwall. So: it is really about time we set foot in this pretty corner of the earth. Here, you can let the accumulated charm of the county trickle over you, because in Penzance you are met with a 100 per cent real, straight-forward Cornwall.

NO FUSS

If you like exuberant embellishments and lovely design, then Penzance might disappoint you at first glance. At the same time, Penzance is just authentic: old and rustic pubs, such as the Admiral Benbow, are lined up next to places like the Artist Residence or Chapel House. There are few secondhand and junk shops elsewhere in Cornwall, but in Penzance you can ferret out real and authentic items. Penzance is full of musicians too, for example at the very hip The Vault.

A LOT TO OFFER

You will find rustic delis or well-stocked book shops. Food is also a theme: the very popular vegetarian restaurant Archie Brown's on Bread Street is a real must according to the locals. As well as the Honey Pot on Parade Street.

SOOTHING REFRESHMENT

The Jubilee Pool shouldn't be ignored either. This Art Deco pool on the promenade is THE place to dip into saltwater, without having to confront the waves. Afterwards you can sip a tea or coffee at Mr. Billy's on Market Place to warm up.

THE SHOPPING TIP:

№56

CAROLE ELSWORTH
14 CHAPEL STREET, PENZANCE
TR18 4AW, TEL. 01736 366293
WWW.NO-56.COM

STECKFENSTERS
CHAPEL of REST
DEDICATED
MARCH 1947
SHELL
Penzance Billposting
& Advertising Co.
POST OFFICE
FOR
MONEY ORDER · SAVINGS BANK
PARCEL POST · TELEGRAPH
INSURANCE AND ANNUITY BUSINESS
AIRAIN

No.56
VIOLETTE PENSÉE
ROUGE OPÉRA
LIERRE SAUVAGE
POUSSIÈRE DE LUNE
La Perle des Encres
CAPSULES OF INK CARTRIDGES £2.50
No.56

CHAPEL HOUSE

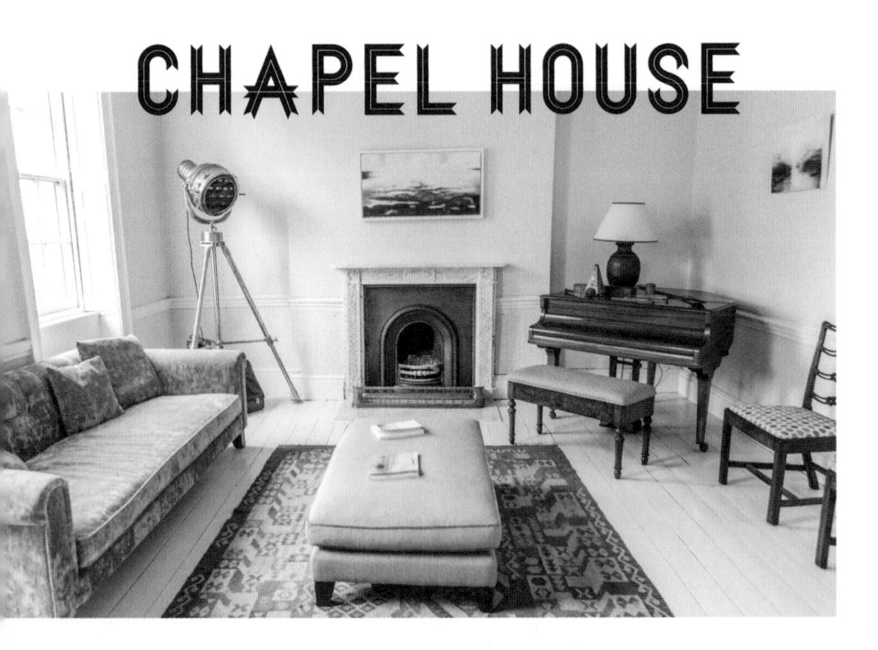

Good taste has a name: Chapel House. Just stepping into this boutique hotel, you feel as if you are being transported to another world – a world that feels like pure well-being. No exaggeration! You can live like a king in Cornwall, in its six double rooms, just feeling glad that you found the place. Sea view and wonderful breakfast guaranteed.

A very good tip: on Sundays there is brunch and lunch available. Both can be enjoyed even by non-guests (upon reservation). We say: a good opportunity to check in to pure well-being.

CHAPEL HOUSE
CHAPEL STREET, PENZANCE TR18 4AQ,
TEL. 07810 020617
WWW.CHAPELHOUSEPZ.CO.UK

ARTIST RESIDENCE

A REAL HEAD-TURNER!

ARTIST RESIDENCE
20 CHAPEL ST, PENZANCE, TR18 4AW, TEL. 01736 365664
WWW.ARTISTRESIDENCECORNWALL.CO.UK

JACK OF ALL TRADES IN PENZANCE

It is love at first step (over the threshold); and even if you can't snap up a room (or are only staying a day in Penzance), it is worth visiting the house – again and again.

Why? The Artist Residence is not only a boutique hotel, but also a smokehouse restaurant. This is what the non-resident guests take pleasure in – as there are many reasons to come back here to Chapel Street. One of them is an enjoyable breakfast. Then after 11.00 a.m., the comfortable lounge with a wood-burning stove opens, where you can read a newspaper with a mug of tea in your hand or, as an alternative, just see what the day will bring.

The smokehouse restaurant called Cornish Barn also makes your mouth water with dishes such as Garlic & Lemon Prawns, Smoked Lobster or Steak as well as Beer-Can Chicken which have found their way onto the menu, giving such anticipation when choosing.

The rooms and apartments themselves don't lag behind, of course. The style is pleasant and encourages you to stay longer in this beautiful hotel in Penzance. By the by, new to this Artist Residence masterpiece is a cottage for up to six people. This is how to really enjoy a holiday.

SMALL, BEAUTIFUL AND TRADITIONAL:

MOUSEHOLE

THE PEOPLE WHO CALL IT THEIR HOME, AND THOSE WHO HAVE COME TO VISIT.

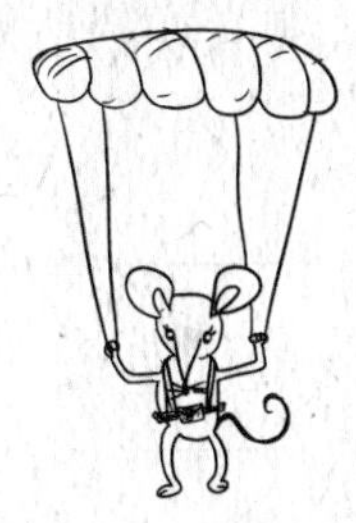

Mousehole is the scene of a wide range of stories. For example, the adventures of the famous 'Mousehole Mice', from the children's book of the same name. Mousehole is also the centre of life for Emma, Beccy, Ben and friends.

Emma Mustill rents out cottages and flats in the area, via Hidden Hideaways. Ben and Beccy Marshall are the epitome of the Cornish surfing couple (blond, long hair, happy and tanned). But these stereotypical characteristics are not the only things that define the two: they run the wonderful shop Sandpiper Gallery, make pottery and drive to Gwenver to surf as often as possible.

Emma, Ben and Beccy are part of the (as they so often are in Cornwall) tight-knit community of Mousehole. However, more than anything, for visitors, Mousehole offers good restaurants, such as the Old Coastguard (The Parade) or 2 Fore Street.

USEFUL:
THE RIGHT PRONUNCIATION OF MOUSEHOLE IS 'MOWZEL'.

After eating, you can lace up your walking shoes and stroll through the town, to be surprised by hidden gardens and unexpected witches' houses. Or you could pack your swimming gear and discover the port.

Mousehole attracts a lot of attention and kudos for its Christmas lights. So for those who have never considered it: a winter holiday in Cornwall is supposed to be marvellous – a stormy sea, relatively comfortable temperatures (by English standards) and interesting, as well as funny, traditions that will amaze you.

EMMA'S TIPS FOR THE NEARBY NEWLYN:

Newlyn Art Gallery and Tolcarne Inn.

Ben & Beccy

810 UYK

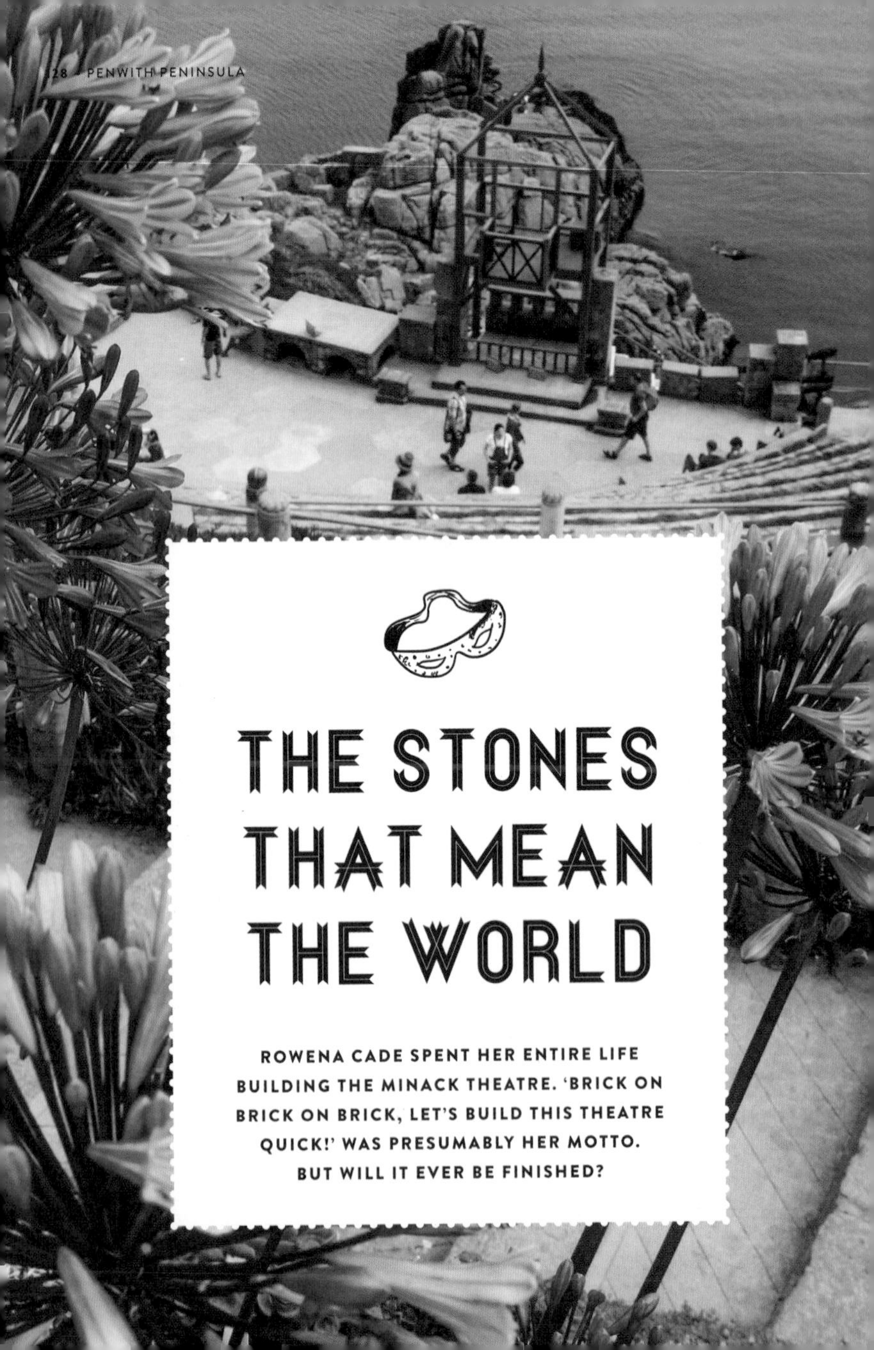

THE STONES THAT MEAN THE WORLD

ROWENA CADE SPENT HER ENTIRE LIFE BUILDING THE MINACK THEATRE. 'BRICK ON BRICK ON BRICK, LET'S BUILD THIS THEATRE QUICK!' WAS PRESUMABLY HER MOTTO. BUT WILL IT EVER BE FINISHED?

One of the managers, Phil, says that the last thing to be built at the Minack Theatre was the backstage area for the actors; they ensure that they have the latest technology and that it is always kept up to date. In summer he works 11 hour shifts, but never complains about it. 'It's a lot quieter in winter,' he smiles. He started when he was a student here at the Minack, to supplement his pocket money.

Even in the 70s Rowena, nearly 80 years old at the time, was constantly building. Her last works were the archways in the direction of the backstage area. Phil's gaze shifts over the scenery of Porthcurno Beach, the Minack Theatre and the ocean. He is probably thinking about the evening performance, during which the sunlight will again fall perfectly on the rocky cliffs, and bring a natural, golden light to the plays that will be staged here. A priceless view. During the 'intermission' between the morning and the evening performance, it is anything but silent. Visitors from all corners of the world scurry around on the stones that meant the world to Rowena, or climb up onto the balcony that Romeo's Juliet stood on, and smile down. The visitors enjoy the sunlight on the seats, into which the names of the most famous plays performed here are chiselled. Sitting on the stone seats, you feel like a VIP, as they are named after stars of the stage such as *Othello*, *Beauty and the Beast*, *Hamlet* or *King Lear*.

PORTHCURNO,
PENZANCE, TR19 6JU
TEL. 01736 810181
WWW.MINACK.COM

WHERE IS THE

MOTORWAY?

PETROLHEADS AND SERIOUS HORSEPOWER FANS SHOULD KNOW: CORNWALL'S ROADS ARE NOT FOR YOU. KEEP A WIDE BERTH, BECAUSE...

... Put simply: these roads are narrow and full of bends. In a lot of villages, the motto is 'twenty is plenty'. Twenty miles an hour is enough and people stick to this. You can probably speed up on the A30, but otherwise it is better to throttle down the horsepower and drive at a comfortable pace.

Cornwall's roads are generally lined with overgrown hedges or walls. Again and again the roads contract into one lane, so you often come nose to nose with another car, get in each other's way a bit and then one reverses out of pure, goodwilled Cornish hospitality. So memorise the so-called 'Cornish Wave' from the beginning: this salute is directed at the person opposite and then everything is fine.

These streets are one of a kind, don't miss them! Here, every car journey is an adventure.

GOOD COP, BAD COP

GOOD COP: YEAH, ROAD TRIP!

A road trip in Cornwall! You can feel the freedom course through your veins. The roads are indeed narrow, but with that, you can always stop and greet other drivers with the 'Cornish Wave' – which somehow works with no ifs and no buts. The thought of narrow roads may unsettle you at first, but when you're driving along, all doubt goes out of the window and every car journey becomes a mini adventure. Anyway the Cornish – even when driving – are extremely courteous. If you don't give driving in Cornwall a chance, then you're really missing out.

BAD COP: ON THE ROAD TO NOWHERE.

You have to do everything yourself. Build the new IKEA bookshelf, cook the pasta and now dash from A to B in Cornwall. These streets are not suited to the modern driver. They are often so narrow, that for a second you imagine you are on the road to nowhere. You can even hone your reversing skills – because you have to do this every few metres, when oncoming traffic appears. One claustrophobic moment after another! Otherwise you creep along so slowly that you almost expect a ticket to be awaiting you in your letterbox, for driving so recklessly slowly.

FRAME
OCTOBER 2014
MAY — JUN 2016
RETAIL

SHOPPING QUEEN

ON GRAPEVINES AND APPLE TREES

TO TASTE WHAT GROWS ON ENGLISH SOIL, YOU CAN HEAD TO THE POLGOON VINEYARD NEAR PENZANCE, WHERE THEY ARE HARD AT WORK FILLING STYLISH BOTTLES.

The Coulson family used to be in the fish business, as is typical for Cornwall. Then they had to move because the family got larger, and the house got too small. The new home encouraged them to cultivate plants, and after meeting an award-winning Cornish wine grower, the Coulsons had the idea of producing wine themselves, in England. A story in which traditional methods and a completely natural environmental consciousness predominate.

WHY NOT?

Despite the occasionally harsh weather conditions every year, with perseverance it has been proven that growing wine in England can be justified, and with good results. This is confirmed by the various awards that the Coulsons have won. It's not just grapes you can press juice out of, but also apples, berries and pears. These are apparently more robust, considering the caprices of English weather, and are a main ingredient of the beloved cider.

WIDE SELECTION

The Coulsons didn't just leave it at cider alone, they also produce the very popular 'aval' – sparkling apple wine – the most popular by the way is the one with a note of raspberry. If this all sounds like too much theory for you – get yourself to Polgoon and join in a tour of the vineyards! There are five tastings on the programme, and because you get hungry from time to time, lunch is now served on certain days (in the form of crab sandwiches or charcuterie platters). If you are inspired by the tour, in the shop you can buy not only Polgoon produce, but a wide selection of Cornish specialties will also impress you.

Cheers!

TIPS:

—

SURF & TASTE:
WINE TASTING AND SURF LESSON IN ONE

—

THE POLGOON HOLIDAY COTTAGE RIGHT NEXT TO THE VINEYARDS

POLGOON VINEYARD & ORCHARD
ROSEHILL, PENZANCE
TR20 8TE
TEL. 01736 333946
WWW.POLGOON.COM

TOURS BY APPT.
WINERY
OPEN 10 - 4
01736 333946

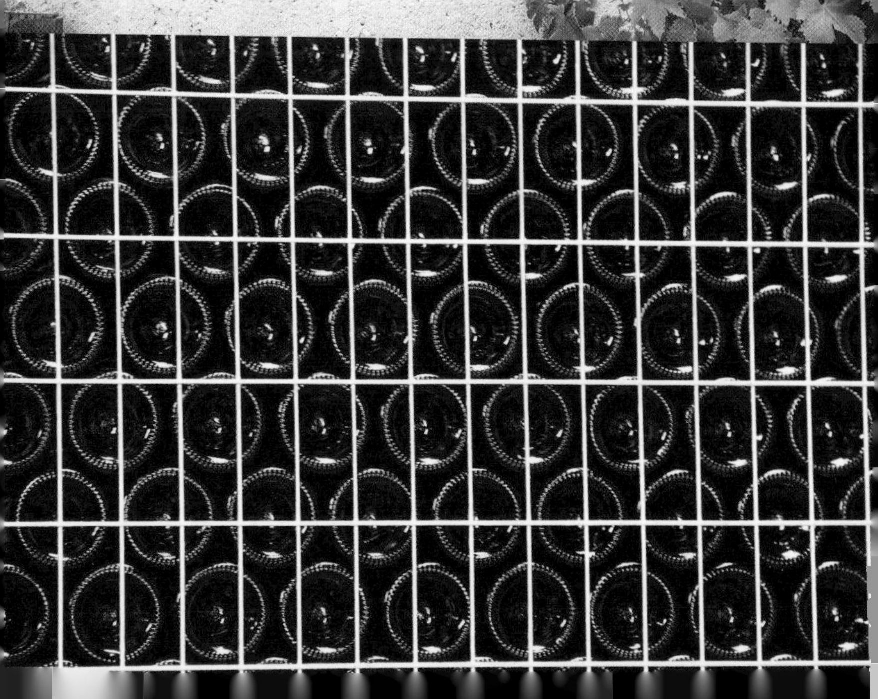

ACTION HERO

A SMALL BEACH COCKTAIL

PROFILE: PORTHCURNO BEACH

When the Cornish go to the beach, on no condition do they forget their windbreak. On one hand, their offspring are protected from the wind, on the other hand, their skin is also protected from the sun. However, their pale skin does not stop these people from outright enjoying themselves: beachball fields are drawn in the sand here, cricket is practised there, someone is knocking about in the waves with a boogie board, or is reading a good book. Admittedly, the amount of children in the (about 17°C) water outweighs the amount of adults by far, but you should still give Cornish swimming a try. Just once won't hurt! Porthcurno Beach, with its turquoise water and imposing cliffs, lined with broad sandy beaches, was simply predestined for you to overcome your inner fears and jump into the waves, like the Cornish do.

PORTHCHAPEL BEACH

Past the Minack, right next to the tiny village of St Levan, the stone steps lead down to the small but beautiful Porthchapel Beach. The locals all love this spot of sand – understandably, because in good weather, the water is turquoise and you are all alone on the beach (especially in the morning). Delightful! However you should bring food and drink with you, or there's the Minack Café nearby.

SENNEN COVE

This beach just screams 'wow!'. Surfing spot, impressive scenery and clean sand. On hot days there is a lot going on here and you don't even need a book, because the most beautiful stories are written by life at Sennen Cove: those of the Cornish gradually turning into lobsters, beginner surfers falling into the water and beach cricket or rugby players. If you have forgotten something, you can get anything you need in this tiny village, from the café (good!) to the pub, or beach supplies shop. The mile-long beach, with its crystal-blue water and white sand, is addictive and is one of the locals' and visitors' favourite beaches. When you realise that the next stop after the horizon is the American coast, you get an excited feeling in your belly. Many coastal walks start here; the one and a half mile long path around the head of Pedn-men-du to Land's End would be one of them.

GWENVER

Experienced surfers and locals prefer the slightly more northerly located beach, Gwenver to Sennen. It takes longer to traipse there, but you are rewarded with even rawer waves and a more private location. Although you should really watch out, as there are no lifeguards here to pull you out in an emergency.

MARAZION

You can easily cycle here from Penzance – and indeed with a constant view of St Michael's Mount. Otherwise you can just park in Marazion car park, then simply jump over the small stone wall and you are already on a beach that is particularly – if you catch it in the right winds – popular with wind surfers. Other than that, it is particularly suited to children, because the water is calmer than anywhere else. St Michael's Mount, where you can wander over to at low tide, takes care of the rest.

LIFEGUARD

ACTION HERO

POLDARK MEETS PORTHCURNO

There's always time for a short walk in Cornwall – because you can always rely on the South West Coast Path. It is cool every time you move away from the frame (the cliffs) and into the picture – as even the inner parts of the county are hikeable.

Everyone knows clearing your head in the fresh air is good for you, and where else could you do that better than on the cliffs of Penwith? Armed with the small booklet *40 Coast and Country Walks*, we popped from Porthcurno car park to the Telegraph Museum and into 'the bush'. The fields scrunched under our hiking shoes as we walked. It wasn't completely clear how the path leads to St Levan, but soon we had the destination – the church – in front of our eyes. The finale through a meadow was particularly excellent. A sneak-peak into the church, granted to us by the friendly parish vicar, put a lasting smile on our faces. Afterwards we went over the bridge to the lookout, better known as the National Coastwatch Institution.

LOOK, POLDARK!'

But wait! We weren't able to go any further. A group of female fans (aged 60+) warned us beforehand that the silhouettes of people standing out on the cliffs in front of the sunset were not common hikers, no – they were in the process of filming for the BBC series *Poldark*. And we were (nearly) in the middle of it. So we turned back and made our way down to Porthchapel Beach, which we immediately fell in love with. This is how a short, two hour walk can really give you such a happy feeling in your stomach – fascinating every time! And we recommend it!

FUN FOR THE

KIDS

THIS IS HOW TO KEEP THE KIDS IN A GOOD MOOD IN PENWITH.

Organise a beach day: Nanjizal Beach, Porthcurno and Sennen (the last two are always looked after by lifeguards in summer).

For big kids: rent kayaks or boats at Lamorna Cove.

Drive to the Cornish Seal Sanctuary in Gweek. The kids' hearts will be completely won over. It will go down a storm with the kids, when they see the rescued seals, penguins and play area.

A cycling tour. Rent bikes and perhaps do the tour on the path from Newlyn to Marazion.

Visit the Minack Theatre: it always has plays for kids at the ready.

Head to the Telegraph Museum in Porthcurno.

is where the remains of a Stone Age settlement lie. Attractive to children because there are lots of opportunities to go underground and hide. If overground, don't forget your picnic blanket!

For rainy days:
Visit Geevor Tin Mine in Pendeen: here you can get a sense of what the miners' everyday life looked like underground.

Go to St Michael's Mount near Marazion or to Trewidden Garden near Penzance.

SPECIAL TIP:

The walk (small hike) from Trevedran Farm in Saint Buryan to St Loy by the sea (one hour there and back at an adult's pace). You can park directly at Trevedran Farm on a field.

CARROT CAKE
(VEGAN)

THE KEEN CORNISH BAKER, HELEN FROM THE FORMER APPLE TREE CAFÉ, TELLS US HOW TO MAKE A PROPER CARROT CAKE.

Cake mixture:

200 g finely grated carrots
1 lemon, juice and rind
115 g brown sugar
115 ml sunflower oil
1 teaspoon cinnamon
1 teaspoon baking powder
225 g flour

*

Icing:

1 teaspoon vanilla essence
1 tablespoon lemon juice
2 tablespoons vegetable oil
170 g icing sugar

*

1. Mix grated carrots, lemon rind and lemon juice.
2. Add sugar, oil and cinnamon to the mixture.
3. Mix with flour and baking powder and empty into a greased (18 × 20 cm) cake tin.
4. Bake for 40–50 minutes at 180°C.
5. Leave to cool slightly.
6. While the cake is cooling, mix the icing sugar, vanilla essence, lemon juice and oil. If it is not properly liquid, add a dash of water.
7. Finally pour the sugar glaze over the cake and enjoy.

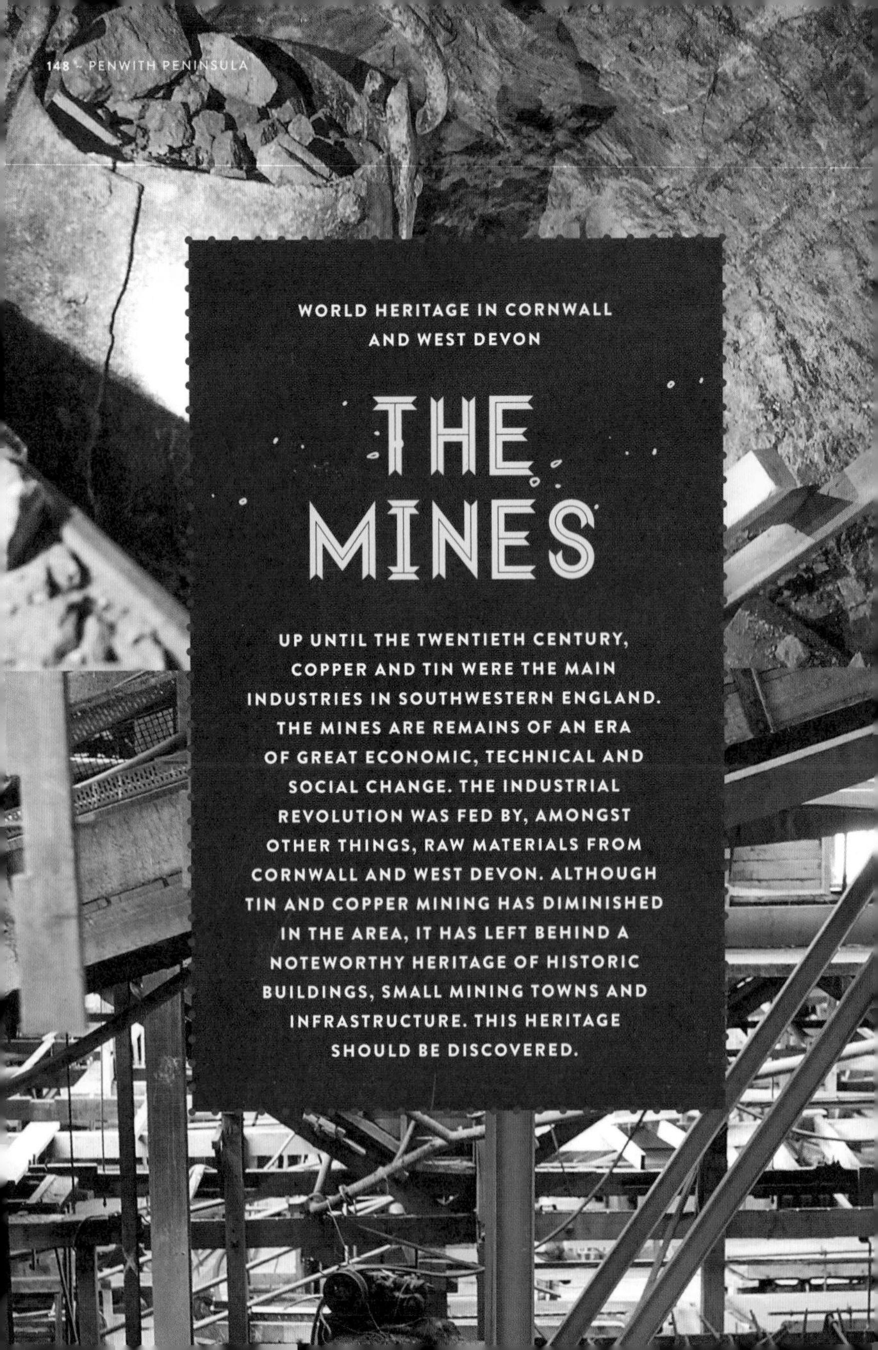
WORLD HERITAGE IN CORNWALL
AND WEST DEVON
THE
MINES
UP UNTIL THE TWENTIETH CENTURY, COPPER AND TIN WERE THE MAIN INDUSTRIES IN SOUTHWESTERN ENGLAND. THE MINES ARE REMAINS OF AN ERA OF GREAT ECONOMIC, TECHNICAL AND SOCIAL CHANGE. THE INDUSTRIAL REVOLUTION WAS FED BY, AMONGST OTHER THINGS, RAW MATERIALS FROM CORNWALL AND WEST DEVON. ALTHOUGH TIN AND COPPER MINING HAS DIMINISHED IN THE AREA, IT HAS LEFT BEHIND A NOTEWORTHY HERITAGE OF HISTORIC BUILDINGS, SMALL MINING TOWNS AND INFRASTRUCTURE. THIS HERITAGE SHOULD BE DISCOVERED.

10 DIFFERENT EXTRACTION SITES + UNESCO = WORLD HERITAGE

CORNISH MINING

- GEEVOR TIN MINE -

THE LARGEST MAINTAINED MINING SITE FOR METAL EXTRACTION IN THE UK.

- Take part in a tour and wonder at the narrow tunnels and colourful miners' helmets.

- Experience good cafés, shops and galleries in the nearby St Just, a former mining town.
- Hike Cape Cornwall and feel the sea breeze on your face.
- Download the audio tour for free and discover the mining area for yourself.

On its website you are informed about the basics of the world heritage of Cornish mining. Here you can find everything you need to plan your trip (tourist attractions, opening times, addresses, etc.) as well as info about current events/tours.

WWW.CORNISH-MINING.ORG.UK

2

– HEARTLANDS NEAR REDRUTH – THE GIANT CULTURE PLAYGROUND

- In Heartlands there is something for the eyes, body and mind: exhibitions on cultural heritage, gardens, a large adventure playground for children as well as artists' studios.
- A perfect day out in all weathers.

3

– WHEAL MARTYN – THE FINE CHINA

- China clay is obtained here today just like in the past.
- Children can gambol around on the adventure tour and in the playground.
- Take a nice walk in the woods and follow the nature trail.

QUITE MODERN: DISCOVER THE WORLD HERITAGE WITH THE FREE APP FOR APPLE AND ANDROID! WWW.CORNISH-MINING.ORG.UK/DOWNLOAD-COUSIN-JACKS-CORNISH-MINING-APP

PASTIES!
TODAY they are characteristic of Cornwall, IN THE PAST they were a MINER'S favourite food.

WANT TO GET MARRIED?
THEN GO TO POLDARK MINE AND SAY 'I DO'.

Hiking and biking along the former rail lines – called 'MINERAL TRAMWAYS'.

You're never far away from the next tin mine.

A POT FULL OF WILDERNESS – A DIARY ENTRY

When I woke up on the morning of the 5th of August, I thought it would be a day like any other, but when I saw Vera's face, I knew that would not be the case.

Caroline alias 'Fat Hen'

THINK TWICE

This morning Vera's stomach just didn't want to play along, so it was scrambled eggs and bacon for me, and a mashed banana for her.

Race with Time

Then suddenly time was short, possibly because of Vera's stomach, then looking for a chemist's, orientation problems, lack of money, ATMs on strike, slow cashiers, just general bad timing. Somehow we still managed to make it, by the skin of our teeth, to our appointment – we were supposed to be climbing through the Cornish wilderness and undergrowth looking for herbs, fruits and roots etc. to cook with the 'Fat Hen'. 'Foraging-Cooking-Eating', that was the plan.

The Latecomers

German-speaking people are notoriously punctual. We two Austrians put an end to this preconception, as we turned up to Caroline's farm a generous 20 minutes late. Out of breath and with the Cornish thickets behind us, we took a seat in the sunny front yard. Caroline was in the middle of describing her background: she was a biologist and worked at the uni, until she became tired of sitting inside for hours and correcting work. She wanted to go outside into nature and use what she knew. And that is the story of the 'Fat Hen' at the end of England. You can nearly touch Land's End from her Boscawen-noon Farm.

Name Tags or... the Adventure Begins

Everyone was given a food label which indicated which wild food they had to forage for. Judging by our name tags, we were the only ones for whom the names of the herbs and other items we had to find were incomprehensible. And that's how it was. What was labelled as a so-called bilberry, was a blueberry; then there was a term 'Fat Hen' used for a wild plant, which was similar to spinach. By the time we had driven to the first forage, it had become clear that we had let ourselves in for more than we originally thought. A second later, the feeling you have when you're on a semester abroad set in. In Tara from Gloucestershire's small, crunching Fiat Punto, we chatted about cultural differences and how important it is to have a sustainable lifestyle.

Fruiticulture

Caroline also works for the National Trust and gives tours of (relatively) untouched areas of Cornwall – we suddenly found ourselves in one of these unspoilt areas. It was our task to find blackberries, which were going to be used to garnish a pie. We chattered while walking with Kate and her friend, who were both very interested in our project. Our getting to know each other was interrupted by Caroline's intelligent input about wild plants, again and again. She even ate a nettle leaf for demonstration purposes (it also comes in cheese here, so it seems to be VERY popular!). 'Just fold it into a very small package and eat it with a lot of saliva, then it doesn't sting,' the self-named 'Fat Hen' tells us with a – slightly – sceptical look. On we went to a wide plain. A dream. You could see the north, as well as the south coast of the Penwith Peninsula and it felt as if the sea was really hugging you. We frantically tried to find bilberries, which weren't easily found – despite the season.

For what seemed like an eternity, we foraged around in the bushes to find the small, round leaves and their blue-red appendages somewhere. And look here – I had one. When this task was completed, we followed the others to the crest of a hill where we came across a group of hungry, wild horses. They were so cheeky and they did not hesitate to help themselves from Caroline's basket.

Horse-Stroker

As they were very small horses, at some point my inhibitions disappeared, and I started to stroke them. I didn't want to do anything else all day, because they were soft and amusing: they even had funny beards! Then it was time to stop and whilst I photographed the ponies with Kate, nearly everybody else disappeared. Only four of us were left and we made an effort to stride back to the cars as quickly as possible. Smartypants Vera and Katharina had decided to wear shorts today and were nearly half-scratched to death by the knee-high undergrowth. (OK – it wasn't that extreme, but it did hurt.) Once we had arrived at the car, we were completely alone and Kate started to tell us adventurous stories about her time in Australia and New Zealand, where UFOs, narrow paths and striking horses were involved. Vera and

I listened intently. Then at some point, it became clear that the others were looking for us four in the thickets, while we were experiencing one suspense-packed story after the other. In the end – about half an hour late – Caroline and the rest were back at the cars and we could eat frittatas with Fat Hen. A pleasure! Accompanied by homemade elderflower juice – I have never drunk a better one.

The Sea

Even right next to the sea there are edible plants and that's why our next destination was a neighbouring area of Marazion: Perranuthnoe, here we got to know black mustard, which tastes amazingly of horseradish and can pep up any meal. As Caroline started on the history of field crops, I was hooked. Which plants used to be grown, such as those introduced by the first settlers in America, who planted them everywhere. These plants quickly earned the nickname 'White Man's Footstep': I found all of this very exciting and I am already planning on buying a book about this subject.

The House

When I stepped into the 'Fat Hen's' house, it became clear to me how J. K. Rowling was

able to write the books that she did. The place looked as if it had been taken directly out of a Harry Potter book. Portholes from the children's room to the balcony, the bannister draped with fishing nets and entire kitchen cupboards mounted crookedly. I loved this house from the first second. Character that has grown over the centuries to which Caroline and her family have added in some small way. I kept on catching myself examining every corner avidly in order to imprint it into my memory forever: you don't see something like this every day.

Caroline cooked and delegated us a few tasks: little Charly put the bilberries in the cake, Greg grated the parmesan and I was hard at work photographing it all. Like a big family, we waited until Caroline had added the finishing touches to the first course: serving mackerel with salsa verde (half-wild) and colourful leaves. And then came what I had already been anticipating: it was also tasty. Wild, and put together from the Cornish heath, these ingredients made sense. I melted totally at the sight of the risotto with mussels and clams, which also contained lots of wild herbs to boot and was garnished with the spinach-like leaves. A tart crowned this culinary adventure, which I can recommend to anyone who so much as sets foot in Cornwall and has the slightest interest in nutrition, cooking and nature.

PIQUED YOUR INTEREST?

'FAT HEN', GWENMENHIR
BOSCAWEN-NOON FARM
ST BURYAN, PENZANCE, TR19 6EH
TEL. 01736 810156
CAROLINE@FATHEN.ORG
WWW.FATHEN.ORG

The 'Fat Hen's' kitchen

BACK TO YOUR ROOTS

RECHARGE YOUR BATTERIES IN AN EXTRAORDINARY PLACE.

Living like the Celts! This replica of a Celtic roundhouse is located near New Mill, which today offers a comfortable place to stay for two – fireplace included! In contrast to the raw Celtic atmosphere you would expect, it is actually rather luxurious. Five minutes away stands the real inspiration for this exclusive accommodation: the remains of a Stone Age settlement. Small tip: it was revealed that marriage proposals are also popular in the Roundhouse. A good omen: nobody has been turned down yet.

BODRIFTY FARM, NEW MILL, PENZANCE
INFO@HIDDENHIDEAWAYS.CO.UK
TEL. 07887 522788
WWW.HIDDENHIDEAWAYS.CO.UK

PICTURE PERFECT

Of course it's the sea in Cornwall that magically attracts photographers, but sometimes it is also worth checking out inland too. If you are walking along the small roads from Zennor to Land's End, then excellent opportunities to photograph the landscape arise. In August and September in particular, Cornwall is submerged in a sea of orange and violet flowers. If a cow also comes into the picture, then it is even more perfect!

ST IVES

Nowhere is easier to declare our love for:
French Riviera meets English grandeur.
Seafood in abundance and surfing culture.
The hub of Cornish charm. St Ives was
probably the main reason for this book.
A must-see and subsequently a must-love.

My dear St Ives,

Every time we arrive here after a long journey, we realise that we really have reached our destination. You, with your grey houses, your flowery window sills and unique beaches, have managed to make us fall madly in love with you, Penwith and all of Cornwall. You are the heart that drives our passion. With your soft light, your early-morning mist and several little shops, where we have spent so many pounds, you conquered us by storm. We, two Austrian travel enthusiasts, who finally reached their destination after searching for years, and cannot comprehend why this magical place wouldn't be everyone's number one dream destination. When we are here, we are happy, especially as our stomachs are also filled with the best the sea can offer. Only where should we go next time? To Blas with its wonderful organic burgers? To the Seafood Café, curiously placed off the beaten track but still equipped with such a fantastic range of fish and meat dishes, or indeed the stylish Onshore that serves the best pizza in town? Even though we have been pecked on the head by merry seagulls on your promenade, we simply still can't forget you. Your artistic aura whirrs around in our heads, your gentle architecture has engraved your romantic appearance on our imagination and the view of the eternal sea, only 'blocked' by the flawless bodies of your lifeguards, will always keep us coming back to you.

St Ives, stay true to us, in bad holiday times as well as the good.

You are our inspiration,
XXX
Vera & Katharina

Zennor, Penwith

PORTHMEOR BEACH

MAN'S HEAD

STEPS

TATE GALLERY

STEPS

BEACH ROAD

ATLANTIC

WEST PLACE

WESTWARD ROAD

PORTHMEOR HILL

CEMETERY

BOWLING

OCEAN VIEW TERRACE

CHANNEL VIEW

BOWLING GREEN TERRACE

BELLAIR TERRACE

AYR LAN

AYR

RICHMOND PLACE

AYR TERRACE

WINDSOR HILL

BEDFORD ROAD

BULLANS LANE

TREVERBYN ROAD

WESLEY PLACE

STREET-AN-GARROW

ROYAL CINEMA POLICE STATION

TRELAWNEY ROAD

TRERICE ROAD

TRENWITH PLACE

THE STENNACK

LEISURE & SQUASH CLUB

SANDOWN LANE

PARK AVENUE

TRERICE PLACE

PEARCES LANE

STENNACK GARDENS

THE STENNACK

TREWIDDEN ROAD

PORTHGWIDDEN BEACH
BEACH COURT
PORTHMEOR ROAD
ISLAND ROAD
BURROW ROAD
PORTHGWIDDEN STUDIOS
CARNCROWS STREET
TEETOTAL STREET
ST EIA STREET
BACK ROAD EAST
ISLAND SQUARE
PIAZZA
BACK ROAD WEST
FISH STREET
VICTORIA PLACE
NORWAY
CHURCH PLACE
QUAY STREET
SLOOP INN
THE WHARF
DIGEY
SLIPWAY
SMEATONS PIER
FORE STREET
WHARF ROAD
HARBOUR
LIGHTHOUSE
WEST PIER
LIFEBOAT HILL
LIFEBOAT HOUSE
MARKET PLACE
PARISH CHURCH
ST. ANDREW'S STREET
St IVES
GUILDHALL TOURIST OFFICE
WESTCOTT'S QUAY
STREET-AN-POL
THE WARREN
BUS STATION
TREGENNA HILL
THE TERRACE
STATION HILL
THE MALAKOFF
VIEW TERRACE
ALBERT ROAD
TERRACE
PORTHMINSTER BEACH
Carbis Bay, Hayle
Gwithian, North Cornwall
HOSPITAL

St Ives has a population of about

11,000

The meanest and most underhand seagulls in the whole of Cornwall live in St Ives.

There are extraordinary **light conditions** in Cornwall and artists still make their pilgrimages here.

If you are interested in art then you are in the right place, because there has been a branch of the

Tate Gallery

here since 1993 with impressive Cornish and international, contemporary art.

Today more
ARTISTS
live in West Cornwall than
in the rest of England
(if we exclude London).

There are
4
beaches in
St Ives alone:
Porthgwidden,
Porthminster,
Porthmeor and
Carbis Bay.

The name
St Ives
comes from the holy St Ia,
who had her hands full
here in the fifth century
converting the Celts.

THE 3

Grill Girls

Photo: © Blas Burger

ATTENTION BURGER LOVERS! AT BLAS BURGERWORKS EVEN WATERCRESS, BEETROOT, HALLOUMI OR SPINACH IS PACKED INTO THE BURGER, ALONGSIDE THE CLASSIC CHEESEBURGER INGREDIENTS. WHO ARE THE CREATIVE LADIES WHO MAKE THESE ADVENTUROUS BURGERS?

THE WARREN, ST IVES, TR26 2EA
TEL. 01736 797272
WWW.BLASBURGERWORKS.CO.UK

Photo: © Blas Burger

Their names are Lisa, Marie and Sally and before they approached the burger grill, they were social workers and estate agents. After having successfully ignited the said burger grill, they have won awards for their high-quality creations that explode with taste. The special thing about Blas Burgerworks is the ecological and ethical conscience that reigns here. The three ladies insist on fresh, local ingredients and in season produce. For example, the salad grown with love and care by Cath and Sally, with only compost from the Blas burger joint allowed as 'help' to grow it. They are environmentally friendly in other areas too: they recycle, are conscious about meat consumption and other topics. Since we are no restaurant critics, we do not feel it is our place to describe how delicious the food was at Blas Burgerworks but the burgers are not short on flavour. We can guarantee: while you may pay slightly more than usual, what you get on your plate is really exceptional – thanks to the high-quality ingredients used.

HALSETOWN INN IS ALSO RUN BY THESE THREE LADIES AND WAS RECOMMENDED TO US BY THE LOCALS AGAIN AND AGAIN.

~

HALSETOWN, ST IVES, TR26 3NA
TEL. 01736 795583
WWW.HALSETOWNINN.CO.UK

MMMM!

Edible St Ives

1.
Seafood Cafe.
45 Fore Street, St Ives
Tel. 01736 794004
www.seafoodcafe.co.uk

2.
Onshore.
Wharf Road, St Ives
Tel. 01736 796000
www.onshore-stives.co.uk

3.
The Bean Inn.
St Ives Road
Carbis Bay
Tel. 01736 791706
www.thebeaninn.co.uk

4.
Porthminster Café.
Porthminster Beach, St Ives
Tel. 01736 795352
www.porthminstercafe.co.uk

5.
Olive's Café.
Island Square
St Ives, TR26 1NX
Tel. 07875 585759

OLIVES CAFE
We are OPEN
Olives
Dish of the day night
PLEASE MIND THE STEP

BREAKFAST TIP:
SCARLET WINES
THE OLD FORGE, LELANT
HAYLE, TR27 6JG
WWW.SCARLET-WINES.CO.UK
TEL. 01736 753696

yummy!

Something happened in St Ives that we will never forget. It was here that Cornish cuisine was finally explained to us. For the first time, we became acquainted with the merits of incredibly fresh fish, local ingredients such as Cornish Yarg, the herbs collected from the beach and juicy, Cornish beef. Drawn in by the unofficial slogan of Onshore ('we have the best pizza in town'), we quickly saw what was beneath the surface: under the Mediterranean guise we found the best starters in town at the Onshore and came back for these again and again. It didn't matter whether we sat outside on the promenade, or right at the back next to the kitchen, the starters had clouded our senses and we were hooked. Hooked to see more, hooked for more sea and hooked on Cornwall. They are one of the reasons this book was written.

SURF OR TURF?

Furthermore, we were tipped off by an unknown local (we are still indebted to him!), to go to the Seafood Café on Fore Street. Simple, bright, wooden fixtures awaited us and before we could get a closer look at the place, we discovered that we could assemble our own meals, from the options on offer. Which meat with which sauce and which side? We might have this nice roll of meat with a thick, red-wine sauce and parmesan purée. Or maybe the fresh fish instead? That is indeed the most difficult decision in the Seafood Café: fish or meat? The best idea is to go twice and try both variations. A fair chance for everyone.

GOOD-BETTER-ST IVES

Other great locations rub shoulders with the promenade: the Alba will play its way into gourmets' hearts with its sophisticated cuisine (including eye-watering prices); the Sloop Inn is everyone's favourite pub in St

Ives and offers a wide choice of ales as well as typical pub grub. The Hub serves the best cocktails in town, as well as solid burgers and sandwiches of every kind. The Moomaid of Zennor will take care of dessert, at the back corner of the Wharf. If you like you can also take away a few souvenir shirts of this local brand – guaranteed a good investment! If the locals are to be believed, then the Porthminster Café (right on the beach of the same name) is the best restaurant in the whole of Penwith, or even Cornwall? You can sit at a table looking at the sea and enjoy one seafood revelation after the other. We tried it out. It's wonderful – the clams melt on your tongue and could not be fresher. All of this has a niggly disadvantage though – to eat here means you have to reach deeper into your wallet and fork out a bit, even if you restrict yourself to the starters. However, it's reasonable if you want to treat yourself and this is why the Porthminster has also won a place in our Top 5 (and our hearts). Note: tables are better reserved in advance.

mmmm!

GOOD ALTERNATIVES

For fans of cake, Olive's, found in a maze of streets is a must: Jaffa Cake, Triple Chocolate, Raspberry Dream, everything is here and of course homemade. The owner Adrian Steeler found inspiration for the restaurant in Spanish Seville.

We also heartily recommend the Bean Inn Restaurant. It might be a 25 minute walk from the centre of St Ives, but it is definitely the vegetarian star of the area. The ladies who run this restaurant (with rooms above) are excellent chefs and their dishes will entice you. Just try it and see what vegetarian cuisine can do!

THE BEAN INN AT CARBIS BAY IS A VEGETARIAN RESTAURANT WHOSE DELICIOUS DISHES BEWITCHED US. PAULA SHARES A RECIPE FOR A DISH THAT COMBINES AROMATIC NORTH AFRICAN SPICES WITH SALTY OLIVES, SWEET APRICOTS AND ROOT VEGETABLES.

THE BEAN INN RESTAURANT
COAST, ST IVES ROAD, CARBIS BAY, TR26 2RT
TEL. 01736 791706, WWW.THEBEANINN.CO.UK

FOR THE MOROCCAN CHERMOULA PASTE:

1 TABLESPOON GROUND CUMIN
1 TABLESPOON GROUND GINGER
2 TABLESPOONS PAPRIKA
1 PINCH OF SAFFRON
400 G TINNED CHOPPED TOMATOES
10 DRIED APRICOTS
JUICE OF ONE LEMON
1 TABLESPOON GROUND CINNAMON
½ TABLESPOON GROUND WHITE PEPPER
½ TEASPOON TURMERIC
1 YELLOW ONION
2 CLOVES OF GARLIC
14 PITTED BLACK OLIVES
1 BIG PINCH OF FRESHLY-GROUND NUTMEG

*

FOR THE VEGETABLE STEW:

2 KG VEGETABLES
1 LITRE VEGETABLE STOCK
400 G CAN CHICKPEAS
4 TEASPOONS OLIVE OIL

*

FOR THE HAZELNUT COUSCOUS:

250 G COUSCOUS
2 TABLESPOONS OLIVE OIL
2 HANDFULS OF HAZELNUTS
1 HANDFUL OF FRESHLY CHOPPED MINT

Preheat oven to 200°C. Chop the vegetables into bite-sized pieces, drizzle with olive oil and roast in the oven, on the top shelf for 30 minutes. In the meantime prepare the paste. If you don't have a food processor handy, make the paste with a pestle and mortar or hand blender. Peel the onions, cut into quarters and add to the food processor with the rest of the ingredients from the list. Reduce until you have a thin paste. Rinse the chickpeas. Take the vegetables out of the oven and put into an ovenproof dish with the chickpeas. Add the Moroccan paste and vegetable stock over the top and mix well. Cover the dish with a lid or tin foil. Bake for an hour on the middle shelf. Serve together with the hazelnut couscous: pour 400 ml boiling water over the couscous, mix in the olive oil and add half a teaspoon of salt. Cover for five minutes and leave to soak. Brown the hazelnuts in a dry pan and leave to cool, put into a plastic bag and crush into small pieces with a rolling pin. Add with the couscous and mint. Done!

... at Bean Inn, they use butternut squash, carrots, sweet potatoes and peppers.

ACTION HERO

Three Questions for Harris Rothschild from the St Ives Surf School

IF YOU CATCH SURF FEVER WHEN YOU ARE IN ST IVES, HARRIS IS A TRAINED LIFEGUARD WHO CAN TEACH YOU TO SURF ON PORTHMEOR BEACH.

How is surfing in Cornwall compared to other places in the world?

I finished school at 16 and since then I have been travelling the world. I still haven't met as passionate and understanding a group of surfers as here in Cornwall. And despite the wild and sometimes rough weather, you can always find a wave if you try hard enough.

Would you say that as a surfer, you have a particular relationship with nature? Do you think about the environment?

I assume that as a surfer or other water sports enthusiast, you have a lot of respect for nature. And this leads to a heightening of your environmental consciousness. In Cornwall we are really lucky that the water quality is so good. The pollution is so low that we sometimes take it for granted. But it's not like that in a lot of countries and you find rubbish, untreated sewage or car tyres in the sea. For example I once paddled past a dead cat in Bali. Unfortunately there is too much greed in the world and too many people who want to make money at the cost of the environment.

Is there something you should have, to be a 'good' surfer?

The most important thing is to remember that you want to have fun and that you can't take everything too seriously. If you bring a positive mindset, then you have good chances of learning to surf. I always hope that our students take away a dedication for the most real and fulfilling sport on the planet.

ST IVES SURF SCHOOL
PORTHMEOR BEACH, ST IVES, TR26 1JZ
TEL. 01736 793938
WWW.STIVESSURFSCHOOL.CO.UK

Photo: © Harris Rothschild

The studio is located in the Sloop Craft Workshops, a collection of small ateliers and shops where you can browse and be amazed.

SHOPPING QUEEN

THE WORLD OF THE MUJUS

KATIE TELLS US WHAT IT'S LIKE TO BE AN ARTIST IN ST IVES

What is a muju exactly?

Muju is a character like out of a fantasy world. There are decorative figurines, as a motif on phone cases, as a picture – there are quite a lot of uses for a muju. The character is loved by old and young and my boyfriend and I sell our art work here in the workshop as well as on the internet.

You both have a proper workshop in St Ives. What do you produce there apart from art?

I also make chocolate that I sell online and at the farmer's market. I mix the ingredients so that you can eat them even if you have allergies. So they contain no milk products or gluten.

WWW.MUJUWORLD.CO.UK
CORNWALL, TR26 1LS

Katie alias Miss Muju

Is St Ives a good place for you as young artists?

Definitely, we really like it here. We love the summer/winter rhythm in this place. There's a lot going on in summer and you meet people everywhere. In contrast, there's not a lot going on in winter and that's also perfect. In any case, we like that we can bring another, younger type of art to this place.

Are there places/bars in St Ives that you can recommend?

We can recommend Porthmeor Café and Seafood Café. The best fish and chips are from Harbour Fish & Chips. For the best pasty, I suggest St Ives Bakery. And we also really like the Digey Food Room.

Katie's special yoga tip:
www.lucyaldridge.com

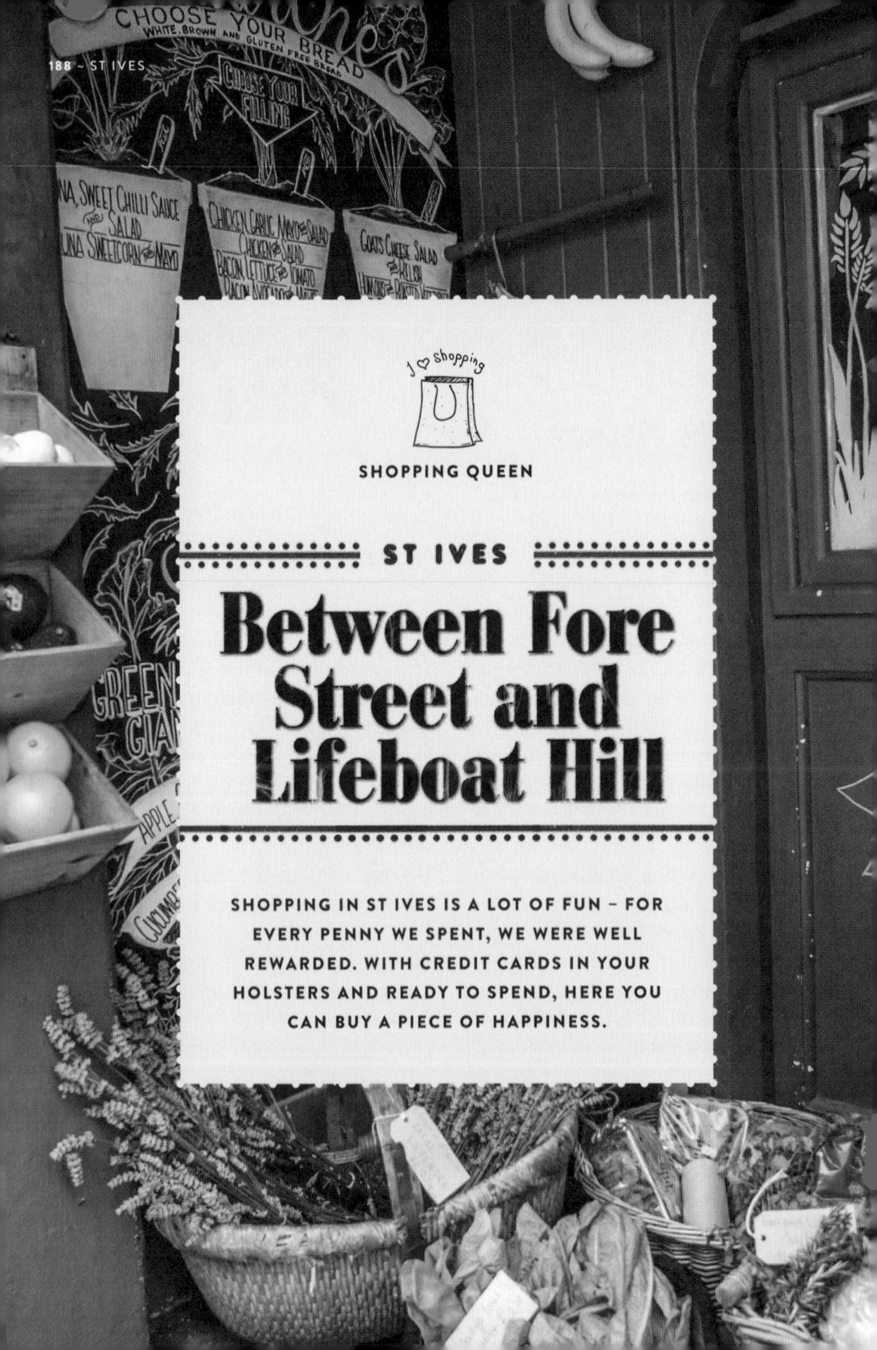

SHOPPING QUEEN

ST IVES

Between Fore Street and Lifeboat Hill

SHOPPING IN ST IVES IS A LOT OF FUN – FOR EVERY PENNY WE SPENT, WE WERE WELL REWARDED. WITH CREDIT CARDS IN YOUR HOLSTERS AND READY TO SPEND, HERE YOU CAN BUY A PIECE OF HAPPINESS.

If you come to St Ives, you will have to keep a tight rein on your wallet, because there is much to tempt you here. Maritime fashion with a whiff of surfer coolness (and a bit 'hipster') impressed us. We shed pounds (unfortunately not weight) especially in cool, minimalist shops like Academy & Co and Port of Call, which really appealed us. If you go up Lifeboat Hill, you will be standing in front of the plastered wall of Sweetlime. All jewellery here has been made by hand, with a bohemian touch.

FORE STREET

On Fore Street, you are at the centre of the action. If you're lucky, you can listen to a soundtrack of Cornish guitar music whilst shopping. Otherwise, keep your eyes peeled. It is better to look in too many shops than too few. Seasalt provides a pinch of Cornish authenticity, a shop that specialises in Cornish-made products – the jackets are wind and waterproof (we tried them out ourselves), which is extremely practical for the unpredictable Cornish weather. Virtually in the middle, sometimes with musical accompaniments, the Allotment Deli is a feast for the eyes. Outside: white hand lettering on a blackboard shows the way to local delicacies and fine foods. Afterwards you find the Common Wanderer, where Raven Williams built his small empire for individual travellers with a soft spot for sustainability. At the end there is – as in real life – something sweet in the form of Poppy Treffry, a super sweet collection of homemade tea towels, cups etc. that are mostly displayed on old Singer sewing machines. Then there is the Cath Kidston branch, in which you can buy wonderfully kitschy, colourful gifts (or something for yourself).

White Beauty

YOU CAN BUY THIS TERRACE – AT LEAST FOR A FEW DAYS. THE BOSKERRIS HOTEL IN CARBIS BAY IS STYLISH AND VERY CONGENIAL. IF YOU WANT TO TREAT YOURSELF, THEN THIS IS THE RIGHT PLACE TO STAY.

BOSKERRIS ROAD, CARBIS BAY, TR26 2NQ
TEL. 01736 795295
WWW.BOSKERRISHOTEL.CO.UK

Established as a hotel in 1931, the Boskerris transformed into a chic boutique hotel a few years ago. If you save up a bit more for a room, you can buy a long weekend here. At the Boskerris, every pound is certainly well-invested, and you feel the luxury as soon as you step through the door of this unobtrusively well-designed hotel. It doesn't matter whether you are eating banana French toast with the best Cornish ham in the friendly breakfast room, or are ending the day with a glass of red wine on the terrace overlooking Carbis Bay: its turquoise and white symphony, in harmony

→

There are plenty of comfortable corners in Boskerris – really cosy.

with maritime overtones, will make sure you retain that sense of well-being. The rooms are lovely, without being over-fussy. Marianne and Jonathan Bassett have taken care of this. We received room number one with a large, fabulous bed and a bunk bed. A rock-paper-scissors game, exciting until the very last second, decided: Vera would get the big bed, Katharina would get the bunk bed. Even the 'kid's room' was perfect to sleep in. Then, with so many fresh fruits (the strawberries even crowned with passion fruit seeds), homemade smoothies and a balanced range of hot meals, all cooked by Jonathan, the motivation to wake up was large indeed.

Marianne & Jonathan Bassett

MARIANNE & JONATHAN BASSETT RUN THE BOSKERRIS HOTEL IN CARBIS BAY AND CLEARLY LOVE THEIR WORK.

How would you describe your guests?

Marianne: A really nice colourful mix. We get a lot of young couples, but also families or more elderly people. We get a lot of people from Switzerland or Germany, by the way.

How has Cornwall changed in recent years?

Marianne: Really quite a lot, but in a good way. People like Jamie Oliver or Rick Stein have brought a younger audience here. Their enthusiasm for Cornwall caused ripples. Due to them, Cornwall now has finally got its well-earned place with regards to good food.

You were born in Cornwall, what's the first thing you can remember?

Jonathan: my grandad's crab business, the big festival on the 1 May and pub visits with my father.

What is special about Boskerris?

Marianne: On one hand, we have a really beautiful view, on the other hand, we are just happy to be able to receive so many different guests in our home. It can happen that a middle-aged couple on the terrace is celebrating their anniversary and we are hanging up a family of four's wetsuits to dry.

MARIANNE & JONATHAN'S TIPS:

- **PORTHMINSTER CAFÉ**
- **PORTHGWIDDEN CAFÉ**
- **SH FERRELL & SON (ST IVES)**
- **PHILP'S IN HAYLE (PASTIES)**

THIS ONE IS WORTH A VISIT!

Paradise in a Nutshell

IF YOU FEED US BREAKFAST, YOU PLAY TO OUR HEARTS. THIS SYMPHONY IN BLUE AND WHITE (THAT CONTINUES THROUGH THE WHOLE HARBOUR HOUSE) IS ALMOST A MIRACLE. SOMEBODY HAS GOT THE KNACK FOR INTERIOR ZEITGEIST AND A SENSE OF WELL-BEING.

~

22 THE WARREN, ST IVES, TR26 2EA
TEL. 01736 793267, WWW.TREVOSEHOUSE.CO.UK

Black and white is so yesterday – today it is blue and white, especially if you are as well-travelled as the host couple, Angela and Olivier. Here everything is perfect, from the breakfast bread toasted for you, to the hostess' outfit, which matches the surroundings, colour for colour. Really large hotels have already been lucky enough to count these two as their employees – all across the world. Then, they decided to do their own thing, and a big part of that decision was so that their children could grow up in a good place.

Angela and Olivier

THIS IS IT! WE'VE GOT TO DO IT!

Then St Ives came into view, with an old guesthouse built close to the water and their heads were already full of ideas. All rooms were torn out and, apart from the outside walls, not many bricks remain where they once were. However, it is all now a harmonious perfection, with 1950s charm and a love for detail in every square centimetre. There is certainly a sense of well-being, so looked after and cared for as you are here. 'We want our guests to feel as if they were in a five star hotel, but a small one,' says Angela. Both think highly of local products, so Polgoon bottles smile at you from the mini-bar and everything possible up to the orange marmalade is homemade.

~

Warning to the reader: when you are back on the streets of St Ives, you get the feeling you've just been ejected from paradise.

~

TIP: THE ST IVES SCHOOL OF PAINTING OFFERS DAY CLASSES AND CLASSES THAT RUN OVER SEVERAL DAYS. THERE IS A LOT OF FUN FOR BEGINNERS AND ADVANCED STUDENTS. THE COURSES ARE VERY POPULAR, SO WHO COMES FIRST, PAINTS FIRST: WWW.SCHOOLOFPAINTING.CO.UK

ACTION HERO

Gwithian Beach

THE OCEAN IN FRONT OF 'HAYLE'S THREE MILES OF GOLDEN SAND' IS FIT FOR RIDING WAVES, KITESURFING, WINDSURFING, LIFEGUARD WATCHING, WALKING AND WHATEVER ELSE OCCURS TO YOU.

Due to the seemingly endless sandy beach, the lifeguards, the holiday feeling that downright screams at you, you may imagine you're in the Mediterranean. Unless it's raining of course, then you know exactly where you are. Gwithian is not just a beach, Gwithian is also a village. It's small, beyond a shadow of a doubt, but oho! A church with romantic graveyard, an old, forgotten pub, lots of greenery and the famous 'towans' (dunes) will enthrall just anybody.

This tiny village with 3,000 inhabitants is also the haunt of camping and surfing fans. Gwithian Farm, amongst others, is responsible for this, with a camping site that is regularly full in the summer months. A big advantage to camping in more southern realms: Cornwall is green. So you can sleep on soft English turf instead of clogging up your nose with dry dust.

Two final tips for landlubbers and book lovers: the Godrevy beach section disappears completely at high tide, so watch out where you camp out for the day. And the lighthouse of the same name, Godrevy Lighthouse, is supposed to have been the inspiration for Virginia Woolf's *To the Lighthouse*. So there are many reasons to recommend coming to Gwithian.

Where? The village of Gwithian lies 20 minutes by car northeast of St Ives.

PICTURE PERFECT

St Ives is just one big, tantalising model so we'll let the photographer choose their own subject. By the way, one good piece of advice is to go to Gwithian Beach which is located slightly east of the North Coast. Many wonderful photo opportunities arise when you park at the edge of the road and walk through a blustery atmosphere towards the water. Soon you are able to make out the Godrevy Lighthouse. An excellent subject to snap photos of, with many different possibilities for image composition. The rougher the weather, the more impressive

Zennor

The true Cornwall is found at the supposed end of the world – near Land's End, the pastures and the teeny tiny village of Zennor are captivating.

You couldn't find yourself anywhere more idyllic than this. On the green fields stand several stone houses that together comprise the village of Zennor, surrounded by herds of cows. Apart from its fascinating location, what makes the place unique are a legend and a true story. For one thing, in the small church at the bottom of a hill, there is a carving that tells of a mermaid, who is supposed to have fallen in love with a young man called Matthew Trewhella. His song alone was what bewitched her. She lived near Pendour Cove, which can be easily reached over the coastal path from Zennor. That's enough about the fairy tale, let's get to the raw truth (of war): D. H. Lawrence lived here with his wife Frieda von Richthofen, in a house built during the Middle Ages. He enjoyed the time there between 1915 and 1917 greatly, visited the pub, The Tinner's Arms, regularly and gushed about Cornwall – as in a letter to the New Zealand author Katherine Mansfield: 'I love it here in Cornwall – so peaceful, so far away from the world'. In the chaos of war, he was accused of giving an enemy submarine light signals and the two purported spies were expelled from their beloved Cornwall. So much for history.

Zennor today: a small village near the Cornish cliffs, far off from the world.

A TIP FOR THE ACTIVE IS THE REFRESHING WALK TO GURNARD'S HEAD. THE BEST WAY TO START IS AT THE RESTAURANT OF THE SAME NAME (ZENNOR, ST IVES, TR26 3DE, TEL. 01736 796928) – THAT, CULINARILY SPEAKING, IS ALSO WORTH A TRY. THE LOCALS LOVE IT!

THE HOME OF THE

Moomaid of Zennor Ice Cream

TREMEDDA FARM STANDS SURROUNDED BY PASTURES, THE PLACE WHERE THE FAMOUS MOOMAID OF ZENNOR ICE CREAM IS PRODUCED. ON THE FARM WE MET BRIDGET AND CHATTED ABOUT THE PRESENT, THE PAST AND THE TYPICALLY CORNISH.

TREMEDDA FARM: ZENNOR, ST IVES, TR26 3BS
TEL. 01736 799603
WWW.MOOMAIDOFZENNOR.COM

Bridget with one of her grandchildren, who loves ice cream

So what do you do on Tremedda Farm?

We have 110 cows. A large portion of the milk goes to the cooperative, that sells it on to produce clotted cream. One of the things produced here is, of course, the Moomaid of Zennor ice cream. This is made by hand on the farm and is sold in St Ives as well as other places. My daughter has an ice cream parlour there. In addition to all of this we also offer bed and breakfast on the farm.

Has Cornwall changed a lot in recent years?

House prices have gone up a lot. Lots of the local young people can't afford to buy a house any more. Instead we get the city people who buy second homes. I don't know what I should think about that... The rule in Cornwall used to be 'Farming – Mining – Fishing'. It's not like that any more. Today we are dependent on tourism and I don't understand some of the decisions regarding this.

What is your earliest memory of Cornwall?

When I was being driven in the milk truck (to go milking) – and my sisters and cousins all jumped on. That was nice – today that would be too dangerous of course (laughs).

What is typically Cornish for you?

Cream tea and homemade pasties. And saffron buns. So Cornish food (grins).

And how would you describe the locals?

Actually we are quite friendly – in the country. And I would say that there are some really good characters and exciting personalities. Funnily enough we look a bit dark. People say this is because of the Spanish that came with their armada to Cornwall.

After this pleasant and interesting conversation there could only be one plan: off to St Ives and to the ice cream parlour. Katharina tried the Chocolate Sorbet and Vera the Cornish Clotted Cream. Two thumbs up! It's authentic and really packs a lot of flavour.

BRIDGET'S TIPS FOR GOOD FOOD:

~

THE GURNARD'S HEAD
WWW.GURNARDSHEAD.CO.UK

PHILP'S IN HAYLE
WWW.PHILPSPASTIES.CO.UK

~

BOOK TIP:

TREMEDDA DAYS
BY ALISON SYMONS
(ISBN: 978-0-9070188-3-4)

Moomaid
of
Zennor

SHOPPING QUEEN

Trevaskis Has Everything

TREVASKIS DARED AND THEY WON: EVERYTHING SERVED HERE IN THE RESTAURANT GREW ON THE FARM, BE IT VEGETABLE, FRUIT OR ANIMAL. THE ONLY EXCEPTION: THE FISH. LIKEWISE, THEY HAVE AN UNBEATABLE FARM SHOP HERE.

Trevaskis Farm is situated just outside the town of Hayle. At midday it is really easy to get there. You simply follow all of the cars heading to the middle of nowhere. Is there anything else? Yes, there's something else! Trevaskis Farm has decided to shed light on everything it grows, to the visiting public. Those unacquainted with farms not only get to know tomatoes, peppers, apples, carrots but also sheep and chickens, as well as learn useful things about how a farm works. If you already know about the farm, then you will delight in the shopping paradise. From crisps and olives to Cornish salt and fresh vegetables: the search for meaningful souvenirs for your loved ones at home becomes downright enjoyable, because you can find practically all Cornish producers here. When we popped in to the restaurant,

it was mainly populated by a more elderly clientele, though this does not necessarily mean it always is. The menu is not at all old-fashioned: the burgers, chili con carne, lasagna, salads and wraps are a lot of fun. In addition, the Trevaskis troupe are very child-friendly – there is even a menu especially for children.

TREVASKIS FARM
HAYLE, TR27 5JQ
TEL. 01209 713931
WWW.TREVASKISFARM.CO.UK

WHAT TO PACK

Despite the palm trees, Cornwall has little in common with our favourite Mediterranean holiday destinations. The weather can be rough, the rain can be hostile and the wind can be mean. Here are some tips for inexperienced Cornwall-travellers on how to hike the South West Coast Path like the true Cornish.

GOOD SHOES

On the numerous public footpaths, or on the South West Coast Path itself, you are best advised to wear non-slip, waterproof hiking boots (in an emergency, running shoes). Cliffs or stairs – that often lead to beaches – can be slippery.

SUNGLASSES & SUNCREAM

If the sun is in the wrong position, it can really blind you, yes (you can hardly believe it) even in England. So sunglasses and suncream are definitely something to pack.

UMBRELLA

An umbrella is useful, a quality raincoat is better. There are good coats – in case you left yours at home – in every Seasalt shop, or directly from the Finisterre experts.

SEASALT ST IVES
4 FORE STREET, ST IVES, TR26 1AB

~

FINISTERRE
WHEAL KITTY WORKSHOPS,
ST AGNES, TR5 0RD

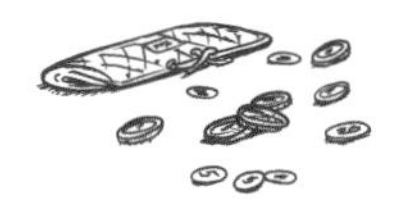

THE RIGHT CHANGE

The Cornish love their car parks. We have also grown to love them. Despite being our enemies at first, they have finally made their way into our hearts. You just have to know how to approach them and this almost always involves coins. This is why a jingling purse full of change always brings happiness. You do have to put the exact amount of coins in the machines, because they are even worse at maths than we are – that means you don't get change back.

TIP: IF YOU BECOME A MEMBER OF THE NATIONAL TRUST, YOU GET A COOL STICKER AND CAN PARK IN ALL NATIONAL TRUST CAR PARKS FOR FREE.

COSY JUMPER

This supports the layered look and helps on windy days.

NERVES OF STEEL

You will need these for the country roads that are often narrower than you would like.

MAPS, SATNAV OR BOTH

'Sabine' (our satnav) was nearly always at our service and navigated us up to the end of England. However maps are also useful – providing you can read them! If you use the satnav, it helps to put in the postcode (most begin with 'TR...' or 'PL...', as the street names often do not appear in the addresses in travel guides or on homepages). Note: even house numbers are practically non-existent but they do often have quaint names.

TIP: GOOD MAPS ARE AVAILABLE AT ALL TOURIST INFORMATION CENTRES. THERE IS ONE TO BE FOUND IN ST IVES HERE: THE GUILDHALL, STREET-AN-POL, ST IVES, TR26 2DS

THE NORTH

All of Cornwall is real, unique and honest. The North is a smidgen more real, unique and honest. Cows and sheep graze high above extensive sandy beaches while inland, cider and cheese are being produced. Surfers are attracted mainly to the craggy, lonely coasts of the North, party people mainly to Newquay. A region of opposites that could not be any more extreme.

NORTH Cornwall

WATERGATE BAY

Newquay

Perranporth

St. Agnes

St Ives, Penwith

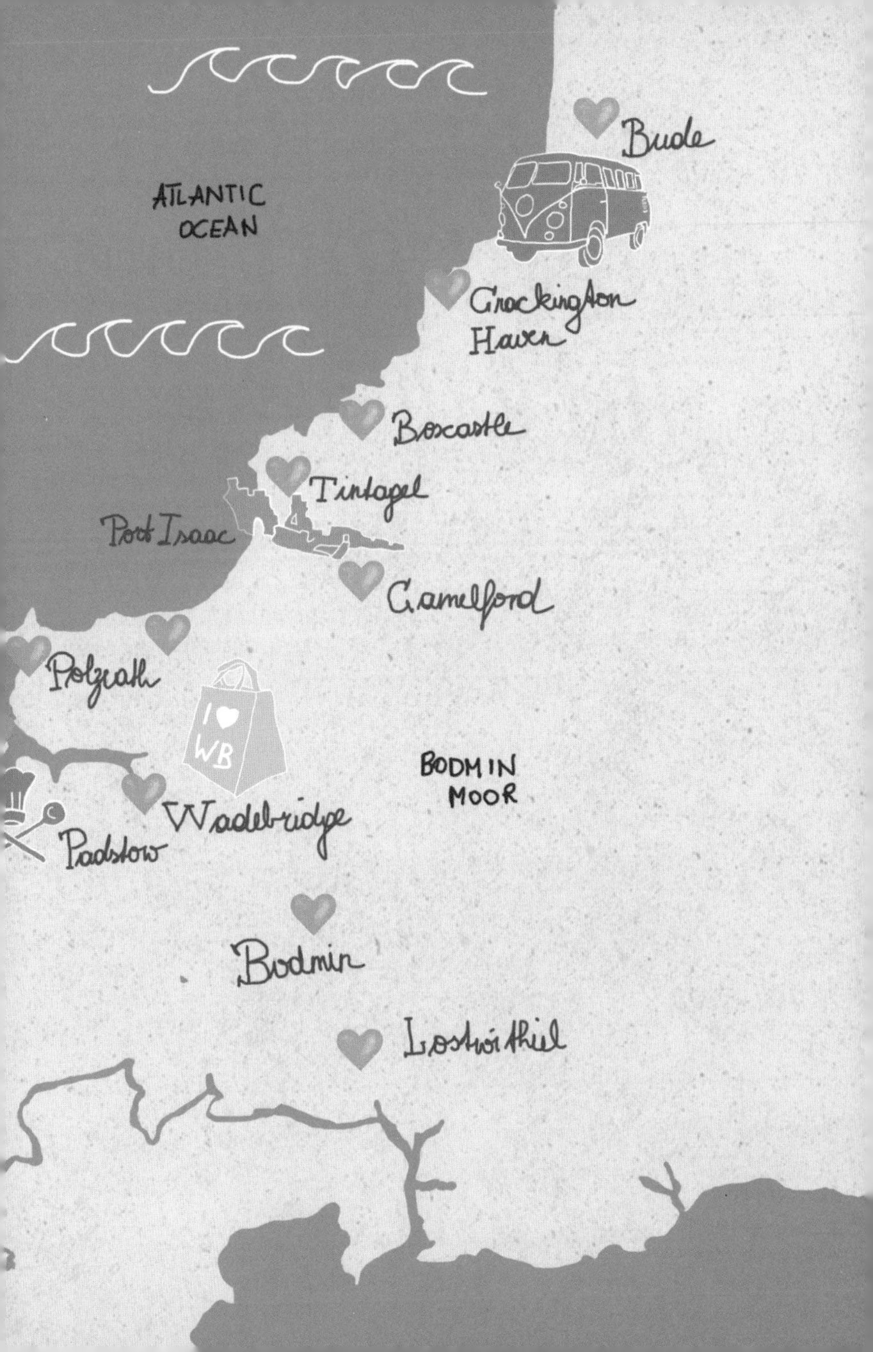

ATLANTIC
OCEAN

Bude

Crackington
Haven

Boscastle

Tintagel

Port Isaac

Camelford

Polzeath

I ♥
WB

BODMIN
MOOR

Wadebridge

Padstow

Bodmin

Lostwithiel

ST AGNES

The Best Tin from Here to Texas

A VILLAGE WITH 4,500 INHABITANTS BETWEEN GWITHIAN AND NEWQUAY. PREVIOUSLY A PLACE FOR MINERS, TODAY IT IS ON THE MAP FOR TOURISTS WHO WANT TO VISIT AREAS OFF THE BEATEN TRACK.

The number of inhabitants is slightly deceptive, because it lets you assume that St Agnes might just be full of ghosts. But it's not like that. During the day in St Agnes, you find a kind community which is spread across the small shops, the pubs and restaurants, or the four nearby beaches. The only people who go walking are those who can appreciate an Area of Outstanding Natural Beauty and world heritage. For many, it is about surfing and relaxing. For others, it is about good food, the people and of course the world bellyboard championships (www.bellyboarding.co.uk).

THE BEST OVERVIEW OF ST AGNES IS ACTUALLY TO BE FOUND ON THE BEAUTIFUL WEBSITE WWW.ST-AGNES.COM.

~

DEFINITELY A HIGHLIGHT: CREATE YOUR OWN SURFBOARD WITH THE HELP OF EXPERTS AT OTTER SURFBOARDS IN REDRUTH.

WWW.OTTERSURFBOARDS.CO.UK

◇◇◇◇◇◇◇◇◇◇◇◇◇

St Agnes Local
Improvements Committee
CAR PARK FEE £2.00
"This ticket is issued on condition that the Committee accept no liability for any damage caused to or loss of the vehicle or the contents inside."
No 56400

Pizza, Pizza!

TO MAKE PIZZA, YOU NEED THE KNACK AND GOOD TIMING. CRISPY BASE, HEAVENLY INGREDIENTS (FROM CORNWALL) AND A LOT OF LOVE SPRINKLED ON TOP CREATES THE BEST PIZZA IN THE SOUTH WEST.

A photographer from London tries out many career paths, comes across takeaway pizza and makes it better than everyone else in the area. 'It's easy to explain my secret: pizza is a simple thing and you can't hide anything, so we take care to use local produce and we have a great oven,' says Jon Crwys-Williams, who takes 100 pizzas from the oven in four hours on a good night. These round delicacies are equipped with names like Wheal Fire, Wheal Kitty or Wheal Busy – all mines from the surrounding area. The types of pizza are also very individual and you'll want to try everything. Ideally you call beforehand, order the pizza, pick it up in the stylish box and walk down to the beach.

Jon & Adam

TIP: THE HIDDEN HUT ON PORTHCURNICK BEACH.

THE CORNISH PIZZA COMPANY
68 VICARAGE RD, ST AGNES, TR5 0TH
WWW.THECORNISHPIZZACOMPANY.CO.UK
ORDER LINE: 01872 553092

SHOPPING QUEEN

Clothes Make the Man Happy

A GOOD ATTITUDE TOWARDS CREATING FASHION AND A BIT OF MERINO ON THE SKIN: THIS IS A GOOD MIX.

COMFORTABLE...

... is what best describes the Wheal Kitty Workshops, a red-brick building with a Volkswagen T1 in the driveway. This is the heart of Finisterre: a small, specialist shop, in which you can buy all of the superb items from the collection for jackets, wool products and surf gear. Right next to it is the office with a balcony. This is where the brain of the young business sits – in the form of Tom and the many motivated employees.

PLUNGE INTO THE COLD WATER

Billabong, Quiksilver and the rest, it's an industry that completely focuses on surfers in warm waters. Flip-flops, boardshorts. 'That's all well and good,' thought Tom – who founded the company – but what happens in the other 99 per cent of surfable waters in the world? In 2002 he discovered this gap in the market and closed it. Creating long-lasting products was close to Tom's heart and he shows a sense of responsibility in everything he does – in relation to the environment and of course the people he collaborates with.

The Finisterre team is constantly hard at work, refining this Cornish brand and

Photo: © Matt Smith

raising awareness about the species that is cold-water-surfers. The wool comes from Merino sheep in Australia, however a large part is also produced in Great Britain – only a few kilometres away from the Finisterre-homebase. These Bowmont sheep provide just as thin and warm a yarn as the Merinos on the other side of the world.

Transparency is prioritised in this brand. On the homepage you can check which steps the products have been through before they are sold in the shops in St Agnes, Falmouth or online. Truly wonderful!

WHEAL KITTY WORKSHOPS
ST AGNES, TR5 0RD
TEL. 01872 554481

~

FINISTERRE – FALMOUTH
(ALSO WITH OUTLET GOODS)
19 HIGH STREET, TR11 2AB
TEL. 01326 318482

~

WWW.FINISTERRE.COM

THINK TWICE

Save the Wave!

SURFERS AGAINST SEWAGE

Sometimes words won't do – actions are needed. And this is exactly where the non-profit organisation, Surfers Against Sewage comes into play. Founded in 1990 by nature-lovers, enthusiastic surfers and passionate beach enthusiasts, the quality of the water on the English coast is at the heart of the matter for the 125 local associations that have sprung up around the country. At organised beach cleans, rubbish is removed from the beach from Scotland to Cornwall. Up to 15,000 volunteers are involved per year. 'Our texts with info about extremely polluted beaches are particularly popular. We send these to swimmers, surfers and beach-goers. Because nobody wants to have rubbish on the beach or, in particular, come into contact with other people's or companies' waste in the water, or even worse: accidentally swallow it,' says Andy from Surfers Against Sewage. This is why they work closely with the Surfer Foundation as well as lead campaigns. The charity has made various task areas their own: cooperation with the government for example, or academic works or volunteer projects. So, a total commitment to protect and preserve the sea, waves and beautiful beaches of the United Kingdom.

Andy from SAS

ANDY'S SURFING TIP:
I LIKE PORTHMEOR BEACH, THE SURF AND THE MOOD ARE GOOD THERE.
WWW.SAS.ORG.UK

PICTURE PERFECT

Very close to St Agnes lies one of the most beautiful and exposed beaches in Cornwall: Chapel Porth. This place is magical for the camera, particularly at sunset. The sun casts a golden light on the cliffs and even the mine towers sparkle in the sun. The sky reflected on the water and the golden light are an inspiration for the photographer.

THE SURF MECCA

Newquay

COUNTLESS PEOPLE COME EVERY YEAR TO NEWQUAY – THIS MEANS THE BALANCE BETWEEN LOCALS AND TOURISTS HAS BEEN SKEWED FOR A WHILE.

This lack in balance is easy to see on (nearly) every corner in Newquay. Newquay is THE surfing Mecca of England. It is the venue for the popular Boardmasters Festival, for example. It is also known as a party town – maybe because of the surf hype, but this aspect can seem unattractive to those fond of peace and quiet. In Newquay you can meet party people dancing in the clubs in the evenings, then relaxing on the beaches during the day.

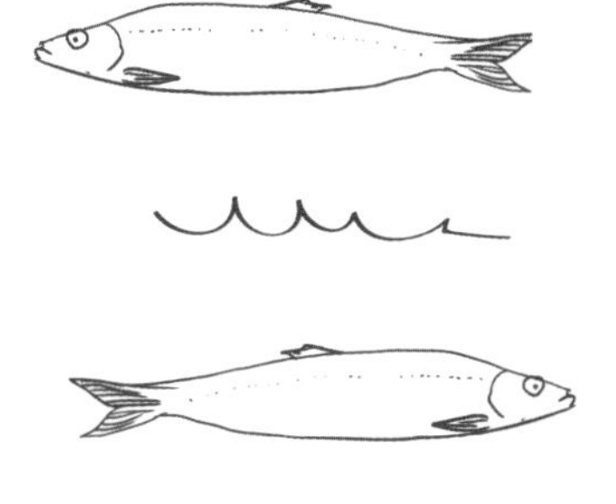

PERFECT WAVE

Nonetheless: Newquay is beautiful – no question about it! Newquay Beach in particular attracts the crowds, because the waves are perfectly suited to beginner surfers taking their first steps into the water. Even bodyboarding is a lot of fun here. And if the water is too cold for you (16°C!), you can sip coffee or cross someone's palm with silver for wares in one of the many surf shops. Slightly more peaceful beaches are also to be found – Lusty Glaze and Porth are our insiders' tips. Apart from the high waves and the long nights, Huer's Hut is also impressive, not so much because of its architecture, but because of the view: from here you can see for miles and realise how many beautiful beaches the inhabitants of Newquay are blessed with.

FOR A BETTER NIGHT LIFE:

THE LOCALS (APPARENTLY) MEET IN THE CAFÉ ON FISTRAL BEACH (FISTRAL BEACH BAR, TEL. 01637 879444) AS WELL AS THE CHY BAR (12 BEACH ROAD, TR7 1ES, TEL. 01637 873415).

SHOPPING QUEEN

A Fine Choice

JAKE AND JAMES WERE ACTUALLY WORK COLLEAGUES AT A COMPANY THAT PRODUCED WETSUITS. THEN THESE TWO OUTDOOR TYPES DECIDED THEY WOULD RATHER DO SOMETHING ELSE AND THE RESULT IS CALLED WATERSHED.

As soon as you step into the shop in Falmouth it is clear: the items on offer here are well and carefully chosen. Woollen blankets from Wales lie cosily next to surfboards from Cornwall and enamel crockery from the Continent. An arrangement of French soap holds your attention for a few minutes, because you just have to smell every one of them – so by the end you don't know which one you should have.

Initially the Watershed boys simply wanted to sell things that you couldn't buy in Cornwall, or were difficult to obtain. Now the two don't just order products that fit their ethos, they have also been producing them themselves since 2015: Jake is the designer and James the marketer of the Watershed collections.

We have saved the really good news until last: Watershed delivers these beautiful products of all kinds – worldwide! Now you can have a bit of that Cornwall feeling sent to you by post, which always does you good, we find.

Jake and James

NEWQUAY TIPS FROM JAKE AND JAMES:

THE BURRITO FROM GILMORE'S: WWW.GILMORESNEWQUAY.CO.UK

~

NEWQUAY'S BEACHES

WATERSHED FALMOUTH
42 ARWENACK STREET, TR11 3JH
TEL. 01326 317771

WATERSHED NEWQUAY
3-5 BANK STREET, TR7 1EP
TEL. 01637 498121

WWW.WATERSHEDBRAND.COM

At Home in Green Meadows

THE ATLANTIC HIGHWAY CONNECTS THE NORTH COAST'S SURF SPOTS WITH EACH OTHER. A NEW SHOPPING PEARL HAS BEEN WOVEN INTO THIS SURFING NECKLACE: HAWKSFIELD!

The first stop is Strong Adolfo's – a great place to sip a coffee. The cake with the white chocolate topping goes excellently with this. Or actually, any of the baked goods. Or the full English breakfast. Or a sandwich. As long as you go in the morning. Otherwise, the pulled pork is a classic that should not be left out. You can chat away the time here – with a good playlist – and not manage to break away from eating, drinking smoothies or slurping tea the whole day. That is, if there weren't all those unique shops at Strong Adolfo's front door.

SUBLIME SHOPPING

It's as if the shops in Hawksfield were competing: each is more unique and extraordinary than the last. You can buy all kinds of great things from kitchen design (Duchy Designs), to select antiques (Goose Shed), to various plants (Wadebridge Flowers). Our purses were mostly unzipped in Jo & Co Home or The Arc (a specialty food store), as we could also buy goodies to take home.

~

HAWKSFIELD CORNWALL
ATLANTIC HIGHWAY, A39
WADEBRIDGE, PL27 7LR
WWW.HAWKSFIELDCORNWALL.COM

~

Trevibban Mill

VINEYARD & ORCHARDS

ENGIN & LIZ MUMCUOGLU
DARK LANE, NR PADSTOW, PL27 7SE
TEL. 01841 541413
WWW.TREVIBBANMILL.COM

Engin loves fishing and the ponds that go with it. One of these ponds – Trevibban Lake, to be exact – is the reason why he and Liz are in Cornwall today. When the land along with its fish pond was up for sale, Engin had to pounce. Grapevines were planted in 2008 and organic principles have been part of the plan from the beginning. Later, apple trees were added, in order to be able to fall back on cider production in grape-hostile weather, as a small and tasty plan B.

Engin & Liz

The vineyard's prizes prove that this has paid off. The red as well as the white wines win prizes and even the sparkling wines are award winning. The white wine Constantine, for example, has won several awards. This wine was named after Engin and Liz' favourite beach, Constantine Bay.

A trip to Trevibban Mill can take many forms. Wine lovers covet the wine tastings and tours of the vineyards. Gourmets will be pleased to hear that Andy Appleton used to be a head chef at Jamie Oliver's restaurants and now cooks at Appleton's at the Vineyard. Holidaymakers will enjoy the four star Trevibban (eco) lodge and sun-lovers will head straight to the terrace with its green surroundings. This is all best done with a glass in the hand.

ACTION HERO

Pearls of the North

THE BEACHES ARE THE MOST BEAUTIFUL SCENES ON THE NORTH COAST – THE SURFERS, SWIMMERS AND HIKERS ARE THE MAIN ACTORS. A VIGNETTE OF THE MOST MAGNIFICENT BEACHES IN THE NORTH.

Watergate Bay

Indeed, the most culinary beach in Cornwall has reeled in a big fish: Jamie Oliver established a branch of his restaurants called Fifteen. Next door is the Watergate Bay Hotel, where you can check into for a luxury weekend, or relax at the bar with a view of the beach.

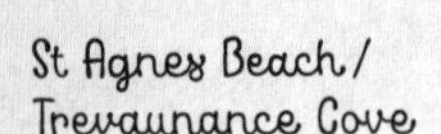

St Agnes Beach/ Trevaunance Cove

At the foot of the former mining centre of St Agnes lies a beach that is loved by surfers and walkers alike. With many cliffs and craggy rocks, this sandy beach has a character that can be best captured in the early evening, accompanied by a beer.

Perranporth

If a beach has been named after one of Cornwall's patron saints, then you know it must be good. This sandy beach stretches three miles when the tide is out, begins at the town of the same name (with 3,000 inhabitants) and ends in cliffs. This beach break is a favourite of wave riders.

Bedruthan Steps

Before you let the magic of this place work on you, read the tide board carefully, because it is easy to get cut off by the tide. If you are aware of the whims of the sea, nothing stands between you and a beach walk through impressive cliffs – except the slippery-wet steps!

Constantine Bay

Large dunes and some greenery frame this boundless beach, three miles west of Padstow. It was this scenery that lured Margaret Thatcher here regularly, during her time as prime minister. Note: the nearby golf course is said to be one of the most beautiful in Cornwall!

CHANCE
RAIN
FAIR
STORMY
VERY DRY
28
29
30
31
WET
OR
MORE WIND
DRY
OR
LESS WIND
FALL
for
RISE
for
Except
WET

delicious!

FOOD LOVER

A Cornish Cornucopia

SMOKED SALMON SALAD WITH RED CABBAGE, CORNISH CRAB WITH WASABI MAYONNAISE OR CLAMS WITH SERRANO HAM. CORNISH CUISINE IS VERY SOPHISTICATED AND IT'S AVAILABLE ON A PLATE IN PADSTOW.

The development from a once poor Cornwall, streaked with tin and copper mines, to the current gourmet and epicurean Mecca is a long one. However in recent decades, one man in particular has fought for Cornwall: the TV chef Rick Stein, originally from Padstow, who first had to earn his spurs in the big, wide world. Rick has become the local hero of many restaurants (in Padstow alone!) and has done a lot for the region and its image. He himself only comes to the little fishing village occasionally – which displeases the locals in particular. How can you be the local hero of Padstow if you are basically never there? No matter how diverse the opinions on the star cook are, this advocate of local produce is pivotal in the restaurant boom and is responsible for the survival of Cornish restaurants.

A VILLAGE OVERFLOWS

When the clock's small hand approaches seven, the gourmets arrive as this is when the top quality and often expensive restaurants open their doors. The little cottages of the fishing town are like a landing strip showing the quickest way to get from the car park, through the narrow roads to the water and, most importantly, to the food. Between May and September there is a lot going on in the food heaven of Padstow.

DON'T FORGET TO BOOK

As tables in good restaurants are often rare, booking is obligatory. In some restaurants, like Rick Stein's Seafood Restaurant for example, you have to book weeks in advance to check whether there is a table available at all.

→ **WWW.RICKSTEIN.COM**

GOOD FOOD IN PADSTOW:

THE BASEMENT, 11 BROAD ST
THE DRANG, PADSTOW
TEL. 01841 532846
WWW.THEBASEMENT.CO.UK

~

PAUL AINSWORTH AT NO. 6
6 MIDDLE STREET, PADSTOW
TEL. 01841 532093
WWW.NUMBER6INPADSTOW.CO.UK

ACTION HERO

Camel Trail

17 MILES FROM PADSTOW TO BODMIN

The hustle and bustle on the Camel Trail makes sure no bike chain remains dry. As is often the case in Cornwall, something old has been redesigned with a wonderful, new purpose. In this instance, an old railway line along the Camel River has been changed into a beloved bike path from Padstow to Bodmin.

It is easy to find a bike rental shop along this route. The trail is also shared with those who are doing without wheels and are walking, or riding horses. This is why there are a few rules for peak times. Mostly: keep to the left!

You should pencil in two to three hours siting on the bike seat (one way), no sweaty inclines await you and plan your ride based on the weather report, so that you are not completely soaked by the Cornish rain (we speak from experience).

SHOPPING QUEEN

Wadebridge

ROWS OF ATTRACTIVE,
TINY SHOPS STRUNG TOGETHER.
A DANGEROUS PLACE... ?

It's the pedestrian zone. A place to be avoided at all costs, lest it be expensive. Also perilous: the small shops with handicrafts and local products. Keep away! And do not come to Wadebridge on a Thursday, there's a farmers' market. If you are coming here with shopping in mind, be warned: the famous Cornish surf shop Ann's Cottage for example has a branch in Wadebridge. Countrywise on Eddystone Road is the outfitters for rainy days. All in all, the various shops definitely have something available to suit everyone's taste and budget.

Only distantly related to shopping, the ROYAL CORNWALL SHOW in June should not be missed. A big agricultural EVENT with contests, lots of entertainment and copious amounts of local products.

WWW.ROYALCORNWALLSHOW.ORG

THE BARISTA CHAMPION

Relish Deli

HUGO MAKES THE BEST COFFEE IN ALL OF CORNWALL – OR RATHER ALL OF ENGLAND. AND HE CAN EVEN PROVE IT: HE IS THE 'UK COFFEE + BARISTA CHAMPION 2008'. SO NOBODY BATS AN EYE WHEN THERE IS A QUEUE AT HIS CAFÉ EVERY MORNING, TO GET THE FIRST AND BEST COFFEE OF THE DAY.

Hugo

HUGO – A QUINTESSENTIALLY ENGLISH NAME, RIGHT?

Well – we would never have guessed that the owner of Relish is half Austrian. This might explain his feel for good coffee, excellent products and good cuisine. (Cough) Seriously though: the coffee at Relish is heavenly and, according to Hugo, definitely the defining factor in attracting guests. Relish is not just a café, but also a deli and therefore offers so much more. The delicatessen pulls out all the stops, offering cheese to sausages to salt – most of it of Cornish origin. Of course you can also get a platter put together and enjoy this in the welcoming courtyard. 'The deli is not directly on the shopping street, it's a little bit hidden and off the path, exactly as a good restaurant should be,' says Hugo. He himself is naturally a gourmet. When he goes on holiday (rarely), he is attracted to Bath 'because there are really good restaurants there,' explains the food aficionado.

CORNWALL IS NOT ENGLAND

Hugo explains why he came back to England, to open a deli that occupies him basically 24/7, after having been to so many international places. 'I didn't want to go back to England again. However Cornwall is the part of the country that is least like England. Does that make sense?' he says serenely. Plus when he was a fresh, new arrival to Cornwall he also had time to pursue his passions of kite and windsurfing. Today the barista champion concentrates mainly on the well-being of his guests (and his family!). 'There's not a single week in the year that I don't have someone sitting in the courtyard. Winter included of course,' he says proudly. Nobody wants to do without Relish in the area of Wadebridge – whether buying a coffee, sausages, cheese, a wonderful soup or something from the daily specials.

FOUNDRY COURT, WADEBRIDGE
PL27 7QN, TEL. 01208 814214
WWW.RELISHWADEBRIDGE.CO.UK

~

HUGO'S FAVOURITE SPOTS FOR WIND- AND KITESURFING:
DAYMER BAY (NEAR PADSTOW), GWITHIAN AND WATERGATE BAY

Classic Olives
Marinated in garlic, Chilli & black
100g
€2.00
Except for loading
CYCLISTS DISMOUNT
Relish food & drink
Cafe & delicatessen
Say cheese!
Relish food & drink

Beef and Ale Stew

FOR FOUR PEOPLE

mmmm!

- 600 G BEEF BRAISING STEAK (DICED)
- TWO LARGE ONIONS (CHOPPED)
- 1 BOTTLE OF BEER (E.G. STOUT)
- FLOUR
- TOMATO PURÉE
- SUGAR
- SALT AND PEPPER

- APART FROM THE INGREDIENTS, YOU WILL NEED A LARGE OVENPROOF PAN WITH A LID.

1

Toss the meat in salted flour to coat. Brown a handful of meat at a time in the pan at a high temperature and put aside. It is important that the meat is really well-fried so that it becomes brown, which gives the whole thing its flavour!

2

When all of the meat is browned, turn the heat down and fry the onions in the same pan until they are slightly brown.

3

Now return the meat to the pan. Add the beer, a tablespoon of tomato purée, a teaspoon of sugar, a good pinch of salt and a generous amount of black pepper.

4

Stir well, put the lid on and leave to stew in the pre-heated oven at 170°C for about an hour.

5

When you take it out of the oven, stir well, remove excess fat with a ladle and leave in the oven for another 20-40 minutes. Leave to stew until the beef has become tender.

Hugo enjoys the stew at home with 'champ' (mashed potatoes with chopped spring onions and a lot of butter).

FUN FACTS

South West Coast Path

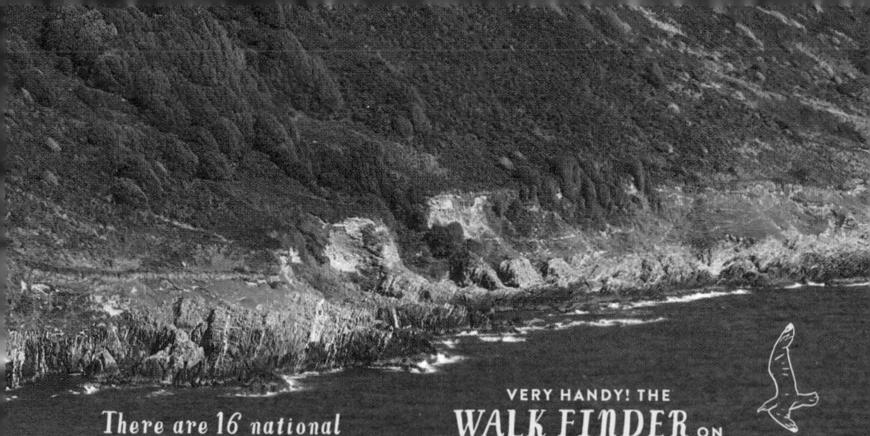

There are 16 national trails in England and Scotland (combined length of 2.500 miles). The South West Coast Path is one of them. See www.nationaltrail.co.uk.

THE SOUTH WEST COAST PATH SNAKES ACROSS 630 MILES ALONG THE ENGLISH COAST.

An acorn functions as the national trail symbol. You should get to know this emblem if you do not want to get lost.

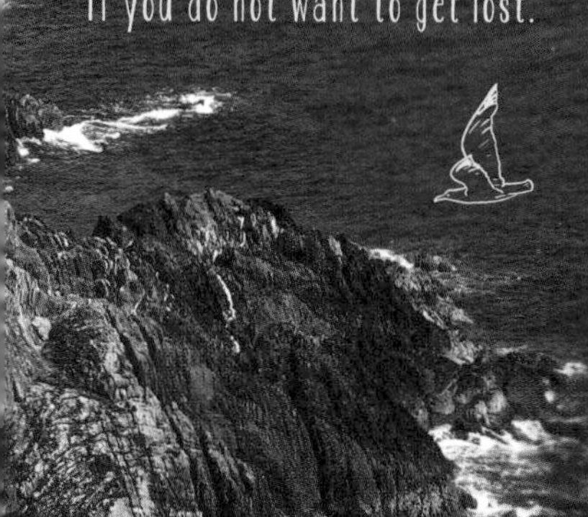

VERY HANDY! THE **WALK FINDER** ON WWW.SOUTHWESTCOASTPATH.ORG.UK FINDS PATHS ACCORDING TO VARIOUS SEARCH CRITERIA SUCH AS LOCATION, LEVEL OF DIFFICULTY, LENGTH OR SUBJECT (CAFÉS, CULTURE OR DOG-FRIENDLINESS FOR EXAMPLE).

IT WOULD TAKE ABOUT SEVEN TO EIGHT WEEKS TO WALK THE ENTIRE COAST PATH AT A COMFORTABLE PACE. ALTHOUGH APPARENTLY, YOU CAN ALSO MANAGE IT IN FOUR.

If you only have one or two days to spare: there are pub walks or wildlife walks available for this shorter amount of time.

If you want to tramp around in your hiking boots for a few more days: tips for walks, from two to ten days, can be found on the SWCP website. For example you can go from St Ives to Penzance in under five days.

WHAT TO TAKE? A MAP AND ONE OF THE MANY AVAILABLE BOOKS ABOUT THE COAST PATH; WATERPROOF CLOTHING AND SHOES, A TOWEL, SWIMMING GEAR AND SUN PROTECTION.

WWW.NATIONALTRAIL.CO.UK

Don't be deceived: the Coast Path is not a leisurely, long walk along the beach. It goes up and down, over steps, fences and across the water, again and again (info about the ferries can be found on the homepage).

If you don't want to make your life unnecessarily complicated, then the **SHUTTLE SERVICE** for luggage will be of use to you. Available along the entire route, see www.luggagetransfers.co.uk. You can also gather tips for accommodation along the way here.

WWW.SOUTHWESTCOASTPATH.COM

One Mud Pack, Please!

STONE CIRCLES AND MANY MYTHS.
WILD HORSES, WIDE PLAINS AND FEW TREES:
BODMIN MOOR IS DIFFERENT.

The highest 'mountain' in Cornwall is called Brown Willy and is found on Bodmin Moor. On good days, it measures 420 m. Seriously, though: it is not exactly easy to distinguish which of the lumps on Bodmin Moor is supposed to be Brown Willy, but it's not really that important.

Tourists haunt the area around Jamaica Inn, day after day. Partially because of the Daphne du Maurier novel of the same name, partially to soak up some of the smuggler's atmosphere and spooky mood around the inn.

What's noteworthy is that Bodmin Moor is classified as an Area of Outstanding Beauty. This means that when you stray a little from the paths, left muddy by tourists' trainers, 208 square kilometres of unspoilt nature await you with otters, ponies, small lakes and the Beast of Bodmin Moor... the latter is however seldom seen...

~

HAVE YOU GOT YOUR CLIMBING SHOES WITH YOU? THEN THERE ARE A FEW ROUTES/BOULDERS TO FIND ON THE MOOR...

~

TIP: DON'T MISS THE FILM-MAD VILLAGE OF MINIONS! FOR ONE THING, THE ROAD SIGNS ARE REAL EYE-CATCHERS AND FOR ANOTHER, A TRIP TO THE HURLERS STONE CIRCLES IS A GOOD MORNING, AFTERNOON OR ALL-DAY ACTIVITY.

Cornish Heritage Safaris

Susan

SUSAN HOCKEY KNOWS ALL THE SECRETS, MYTHS AND LEGENDS OF THE NORTH.

TEL. 07793 743337
CORNISHHERITAGESAFARIS.CO.UK

Dear Susan,

Thank you again for driving us in your Land Rover through the paranormal la-la land. By the way, we will henceforth use the term 'la-la land' when we are talking about this mystical area around Tintagel, steeped in history and superstition – we really liked the expression. For example when we were in the old St Materiana's Church, during the clash and clamour of the storm – that was truly exceptional – and so were your stories about religions and King Arthur... You can read a lot about King Arthur's and Merlin's Tintagel and the many sagas and legends... but hearing these tales with various side stories and links whilst in Tintagel was definitely something else!

mmmm...

The 600 year old post office in Tintagel alone really struck us. Particularly the stories of ghosts and Halloween happenings. And you and your good friend, who works for the National Trust, are hilarious. We've only found this much British humour in *Monty Python*! St Nectan's magical waterfall seems to be a place you don't just stumble across by yourself, so too the Cornish Heritage Safaris. So we will pass the word on and, the next time we visit, you can put us down for the Bodmin Moor tour!

Love from Austria,

Vera & Katharina

P.s. Thanks for the maxim: 'The weather in the North is not "bad", it's just dramatic and better for surfing.'

UNFORGETTABLY GOOD!

CHARLIE'S CAFÉ DELI
FORE STREET
TINTAGEL, PL34 0DA
TEL. 01840 779500
WWW.CHARLIES.CAFE

THE
WELLINGTO
HOTEL
THE OLD MILL
Gallery and Shops
ON FOUR FLOORS
Refreshments
Antiques

Boscastle

WHERE THE WITCHES LIVE

Nowhere else in the world is there so much witch paraphernalia as in Boscastle, because everything enchanting and bewitching has already been collected and is exhibited here in the Museum of Witchcraft (in the middle of the tiny village – hard to miss!). If you learn too much about it, it's easy to get scared. Not because of the witches and wizards, but more the 'normal' people who hunted and convicted the former.

THE WITCHCRAFT MUSEUM

The eccentric museum is indeed the village's main attraction, but it's not the only reason worth coming here for. The car park is run by the National Trust, which means you can assume that nature will feature largely in Boscastle. The often storm-tossed natural port or the old stone cottages near the water are prime examples. You can also hike from Tintagel, over the South West Coast Path to Boscastle if you like. Incidentally, the village was damaged by a tsunami-esque storm in 2004 – in the museum you can still see the markers showing how high the water levels were in the houses. However the village has fortunately since recovered well.

LIFE'S A BEACH

Bude

WHERE THE POLO SHIRT-DONNING GOLFERS MEET THE STEELY SURFERS – IT HAS TO BE BUDE.

his town combines traditional English
each culture, complete with rock pools,
straightforward surf culture and constantly
salty hair. The wind blows merrilly in your
ace in Bude – and this is fine, otherwise
he town would have a different character.
This blustery place attracts a lot of swell-
searchers to the 'first Cornish station' on
he way to the Southwest. Practically on
he doorstep of Devon, with an unsettled
sea and cliffs over 100 metres high, surfers
eel comfortable in their neoprene wetsuits
or munching at Life's a Beach. The golf
course (with a view of the sea) does split
he town into two halves, but this doesn't
bother anyone in the slightest. Not even the
children, who already spend a lot of time
at the beach in primary school, learning to
surf or the basic rules of being a lifeguard
- because nothing is as hip as killing time
at the beach, in a red and yellow lifeguard
umper. If you are terrified of high waves,
but not of cold water, then you can throw
yourself into the tide pool in the middle of
Bude. This tidal basin is also a safe place to
go swimming with the kids.

FANTASTIC ALTERNATIVE BEACHES ARE:

DUCKPOOL, NORTHCOTT MOUTH AS WELL AS CROOKLETS (A SWELL SWELL INCLUDED!) AND SUMMERLEAZE. THIS IS WHERE LIFE'S A BEACH IS LOCATED – IT DISHES UP BISTRO SANDWICHES, BURGERS AND OTHER SNACKS THROUGHOUT THE DAY, BUT TRANSFORMS ITSELF INTO A PLACE FOR A FANCY DINNER AT NIGHT.

TEL. 01288 355222
WWW.LIFESABEACH.INFO

GREAT FOOD FROM A SMALL KITCHEN

The Campervan Cook

HE'S AN AUTHOR AND A BBC2 PRESENTER. MARTIN IS GOOD AT WRITING. HE IS A TRAINED BARISTA AND LIFEGUARD. AND HE'S GOOD AT COOKING. THE UNIQUE THING: HE DOES THIS IN A VW CAMPERVAN.

He would rather look for wild food. For example you can find perfect mussels on beaches with clean sea water. He writes about these and much more in his cookbooks, which we have taken as an inspiration and instruction for cooking healthy, modern and good quality food, in a van, ever since.

WWW.MARTINDOREY.COM

Martin lives with his family in North Cornwall, as a surfer would, because the crashing of the waves is just so seductive. He also has a penchant for this particular kind of lifestyle where the outdoors, good food and a bit of adventure are important. As a lover of good quality food, Martin found no joy in the camping Briton's go-to meal of canned baked beans and lukewarm toast. No thanks.

TIP:
UNDER #2MINUTEBEACHCLEAN, MARTIN DOREY SET THE BALL ROLLING BY ENCOURAGING PEOPLE WHO LIVE AT THE COAST, TO SET ASIDE TWO MINUTES OF THEIR BEACH VISIT TO PICK UP RUBBISH. GOOD IDEA!

Sandymouth Beach

GETTING TO Cornwall

VIA THE CLOUDS

Newquay is home to Cornwall's airport, so it is best to book a direct flight there. Apart from Newquay, there are also London, Bristol, Plymouth as well as Exeter, as destination airports – perhaps with connecting flights to Newquay.

ARRIVING BY RAIL

If you arrive in London – it is easy: you can get on the train and set off to Cornwall via Reading. The advantage of this connection is that you don't have to travel into London and only have to change trains once. Even from Paddington station in central London you can reach several places in this popular county. Journey time: depending on the route and destination, it can take from four to seven hours.

BY BOAT

Many ferries cross to the green British isles – for example from Spain, France, Belgium, the Netherlands, Norway or Ireland.

IN THE CAR I AM THE CAPTAIN!

Renting a car is one of the cheapest options for travelling in England. Plan a four to five hour drive from London.

DOUBLEDECKER FUN

You can also reach Cornwall by bus from various destinations in Britain/Europe.

WWW.TRAVELINESW.COM
WWW.NATIONALEXPRESS.COM

IN THE LAND OF THE CORNISH

If you only want to spend time in one place in Cornwall, then you can do without a car and access Cornwall by public transport.

You can get around by bus and by train, but remember to check the respective schedules with the service providers or tourist information centres.

In a country of camping fans you can rent a home on wheels in various places – old VW vans are particularly popular here. Just search 'Campervan Hire Cornwall' online and Bob's your uncle.

The Great Longing

SHOPPING QUEEN

No herb has been grown that can stop wanderlust, but there is something for lovers of Cornwall who live on the Continent. This online shop is called Cornwallicious and offers the best ingredients from Southwest England.

Cornwall should actually come with a warning: 'Careful! It is all too easy to fall in love with this corner of the world.' If this (falling in love) happens then it is hard to shake off, as you constantly want to return to the land of hydrangeas and wonderfully beautiful beaches. Next to the scenery and the good air it is, above all, the people and their ideas that you will miss. And the food of course.

Owner Jens Putzier must have thought to himself: 'I will help others and start a delivery service of Cornish products.' He fittingly named his online shop Cornwallicious and this is where you can find everything that makes a Cornwall enthusiast's heart race. For example the Cornish seasalt in all forms, from lemon & thyme to garlic, all the way to chilli. Sarah & Finn's Relish and Cornishware are also available here.

TAKE A LOOK ON:
WWW.CORNWALLICIOUS.COM

~

READ MORE CORNWALL!

Book Tips

AS WELL AS GOOD WEBSITES AND BLOGS

Title	Author	Publisher
LONELY PLANET DEVON & CORNWALL TRAVEL GUIDE	Oliver Berry, Belinda Dixon	Lonely Planet
CORNWALL: 40 COAST & COUNTRY WALKS	Keith Fergus	Pocket Mountains Ltd
THE GREAT CORNISH FOOD BOOK	Ruth Huxley	Cornish Food & Drink Ltd
CORNWALL. SLOW TRAVEL: LOCAL, CHARACTERFUL GUIDES TO BRITAIN'S SPECIAL PLACES	Kirsty Fergusson	Bradt Travel Guides Ltd.
TIME OUT DEVON & CORNWALL	–	Time Out Guides
THE LITTLE BOOK OF CORNWALL	Emma Mansfield	Lovely Little Books
SALTWATER KITCHEN COOKBOOK	Louise Searle, Hayley Spurway	Muse Media
COUNTRY	Jasper Conran	Conran

Websites

VISITCORNWALL.COM
CORNISH-MINING.ORG.UK
SOUTHWESTCOASTPATH.ORG.UK
NATIONALTRAIL.CO.UK
CORNWALLAIRPORTNEWQUAY.COM
SECRETBEACHES.CO.UK
LOWPRESSURE.CO.UK
HOSTELBOOKERS.COM
FOREVERCORNWALL.CO.UK

Blogs

THECORNISHLIFE.CO.UK
BAREFOOTCORNWALL.COM
MARTINDOREY.COM

THE CAMPER VAN COAST: COOKING, EATING, LIVING THE LIFE	Martin Dorey & Sarah Randell	Hodder & Stoughton
THE CAMPER VAN COOK BOOK: LIFE ON 4 WHEELS, COOKING ON 2 RINGS	Martin Dorey & Sarah Randell	Saltyard Books
THE WORLD STORMRIDER GUIDE (VOLUME ONE)	Antony Colas & Bruce Sutherland	Low Pressure Publishing
SUMMER IN FEBRUARY	Jonathan Smith	Abacus
REBECCA	Daphne du Maurier	Various

IF YOU WANT TO BEAM YOURSELF TO CORNWALL MUSICALLY, THEN LISTEN TO OUR PLAYLIST ON SPOTIFY: EAT SURF LIVE

AS WE WERE ASKING DIRECTIONS, WE MET THESE SINISTER FELLOWS.

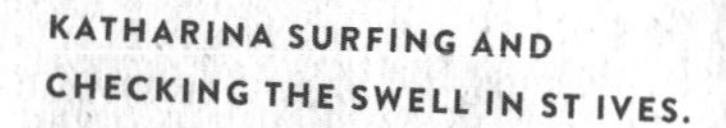

KATHARINA SURFING AND CHECKING THE SWELL IN ST IVES.

REGARDLESS OF THE STORM AND RAIN, WE BRAVELY SCRIBBLE DOWN WHAT SUSAN FROM CORNISH HERITAGE SAFARIS TELLS US ABOUT KING ARTHUR.

WE FOUND OUR TEA RATIONS FOR THE NEXT TEN YEARS.

IN PHOTO ACTION: SEVERAL EYE-WITNESSES HAVE REPORTED SIGHTING KATHARINA LIKE THIS AT VARIOUS SCENES IN CORNWALL.

THE LARGEST FLIP-FLOP IN THE WORLD IS IN NEWQUAY!

WELL, WHO DO WE HAVE HERE? *EAT BIKE LIVE* (THE SYLT TRAVEL BOOK) INSPIRATION, ON HOLIDAY IN CORNWALL.

IS THIS LITTLE TRACTOR IN CADGWITH LOST? WHO WILL HELP HIM OUT OF THIS MUD(DLE)?

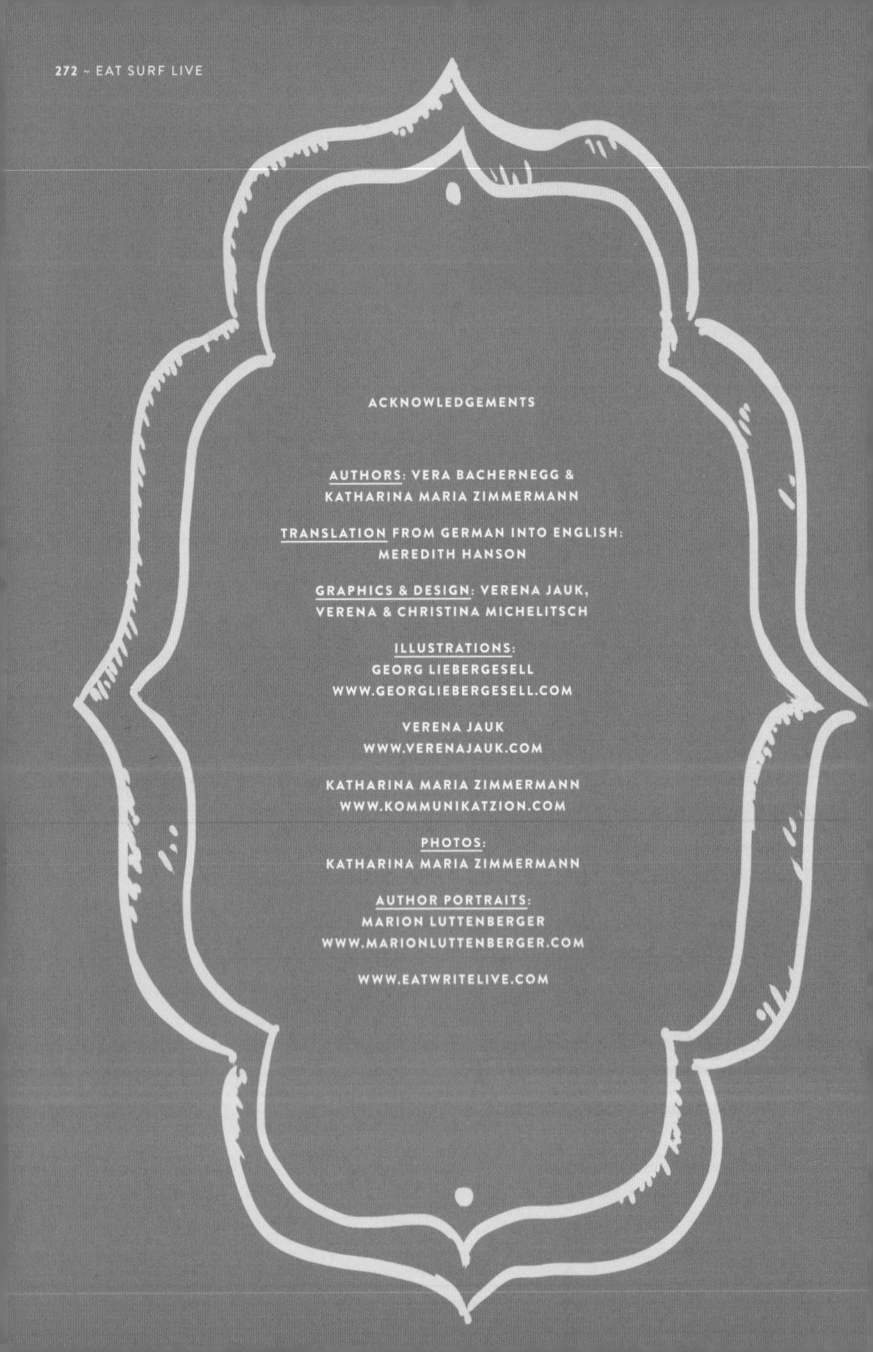

ACKNOWLEDGEMENTS

AUTHORS: VERA BACHERNEGG &
KATHARINA MARIA ZIMMERMANN

TRANSLATION FROM GERMAN INTO ENGLISH:
MEREDITH HANSON

GRAPHICS & DESIGN: VERENA JAUK,
VERENA & CHRISTINA MICHELITSCH

ILLUSTRATIONS:
GEORG LIEBERGESELL
WWW.GEORGLIEBERGESELL.COM

VERENA JAUK
WWW.VERENAJAUK.COM

KATHARINA MARIA ZIMMERMANN
WWW.KOMMUNIKATZION.COM

PHOTOS:
KATHARINA MARIA ZIMMERMANN

AUTHOR PORTRAITS:
MARION LUTTENBERGER
WWW.MARIONLUTTENBERGER.COM

WWW.EATWRITELIVE.COM

Ivanhoe
Sir. W. Scott
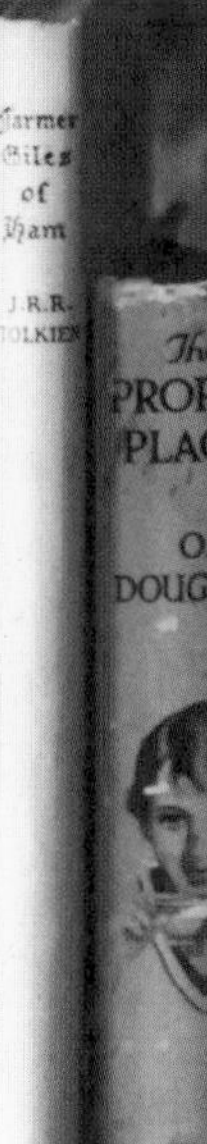
Farmer
Giles
of
Ham
J.R.R.
TOLKIEN
ALLEN &
UNWIN
HOUGHTON
MIFFLIN

The
PROPER
PLACE
O.
DOUGLAS
1/6
NET
NELSON
PAUL
MEGGITT'S
DELU-
SION

JOHN
STERLING
THOMAS
CARLYLE

WILD
FLOWERS

FIRST SERIES

Eat Write Live

The best journeys are when you visit friends, who give you insider's tips and places that the locals swear by. These books from the self-publishing company in Graz (Austria) fulfill exactly this purpose. They introduce the travellers to people, they preselect the most beautiful spots and tell exciting stories that help you understand the country and its people. All of this with a touch of environmental sustainability. With the help of hand-drawn maps, personal photos and exciting design it is always a pleasure to pick up books in this series for a browse, or to draw inspiration for your next holiday. Easy!

WWW.EATWRITELIVE.COM

IF YOU'RE INTERESTED IN FINDING OUT MORE ABOUT OUR BOOKS, FIND US ON FACEBOOK AT **SUMMERSDALE PUBLISHERS** AND FOLLOW US ON TWITTER AT **@SUMMERSDALE**.

WWW.SUMMERSDALE.COM